MUSINGS

OF A

GHOST MOTHER

LOSING AN INFANT TO CLOSED ADOPTION

ISBN 1-930002-29-7

I & L PUBLISHING
174 OAK DR. PKWY.
OROVILLE, CA 95966
PH: (530) 589-5048
FX: (530) 589-3551
E-MAIL: inlpublisher@jps.net

FIRST EDITION

FOR ORDERING AND DISTRIBUTION CONTACT
I & L PUBLISHING

COVER DESIGN BY PAUL CAMPBELL
PHOTOGRAPH BY SARAH VALIM

Printed in the United States by Morris Publishing • 3212 East Highway 30
Kearney, NE • 68847 • 1-800-650-7888

DEDICATION

To my husband, children and extended family:

> I celebrate your presence in my life! Whether we are
> connected by birth, marriage, kinship or friendship,
> your love sustains me.

❀

ACKNOWLEDGMENTS

I am indebted to the fifty-four women who participated in my doctoral research on the long-term effects of surrendering an infant for adoption. This study was the catalyst for *Musings of a Ghost Mother*. My deepest gratitude is extended to these women who shared, with courage and generosity, the impact of relinquishment on their lives.

I was fortunate to have discovered, in the beginning of my own journey to healing, *The Adoption Triangle* authored by Arthur D. Sorosky, M.D., Annette Baran, M.S.W. and Reuben Pannor, M.S.W. These were the first researchers to ask birth parents about long term effects of relinquishment. I remember reading the comments from these parents in stunned gratitude, seeing in print for the first time attention to the feelings of birth mothers and fathers. I thank these authors for their work, which affirmed my reality when I most needed it. I am also so thankful that further along in my journey I found Rickie Solingers's book *Wake Up Little Susie: Single Pregnancy and Race before Roe w. Wade*. Reading Solinger's analysis of how race, class and gender dictated the public response to "unwed pregnancy" helped me understand relinquishment in a social and historical context. This enabled me to make greater sense out of my own experience, marking another personal turning point.

There will always be a special place in my heart for the agency that matched my daughter and me, resulting in our reunion twenty-six years after I relinquished her for adoption. Although we spoke on the telephone only one time, I will never forget that brief and wonderful conversation with Tony Vilardi, the director of International Soundex Reunion Registry. I thank him and ISRR for their work on behalf of separated persons who long to be connected again.

I gratefully acknowledge the talented and dedicated people who work on adoption reform, including the efforts being made across the United States to unseal adoption records so that adult adoptees are afforded the right taken for granted by the rest of the population: to know the names of the people who gave them life. A great majority of birth mothers support this effort; most of us did not ask for secrecy from our own children.

My heartfelt gratitude goes to all who offered me encouragement in the years prior to reunion with my daughter. Your gentle understanding lightened my spirit, lessened my aloneness and helped me move forward with hope.

Finally, and most of all, I thank my husband and life partner, Tony Valim, for his unwavering support, wisdom, and love.

CONTENTS

PRELUDE

When I returned almost thirty years later to look at the Florence Crittenden Home for Unwed Mothers in Washington, D.C., it had disappeared. Overlooking Reservoir Road, alongside the Potomac River, the imposing stone and brick fortress-like structure still stood. The maternity home where I had waited to give birth to my first child had been replaced by a blood bank, according to the sign in front.

Only in my mind's eye would I see a pregnant girl or two, out for a walk, away from the scrutiny of social workers or the other residents, all banished from home and community. Remembering the girl I had been: her loneliness, sadness, bitterness, her profound guilt and shame, praying daily for courage and for guidance to do the right thing. Remembering the one "spiritual" consultation with the home's chaplain and his inquiry about my plans once my baby was born and relinquished to a waiting couple for adoption. "Do you really think you can go back to being a college girl?" he had smirked.

Odd to consider the disappearance of this shelter for unwed pregnant girls, the very concept now an anachronism hearkening back to another time and place.

NOTE TO READERS

Recording my random musings was initially a way to externalize thoughts that would occasionally arise as I remembered my first pregnancy and its aftermath, including reunion twenty-six years later with the daughter I had surrendered for adoption. Writing also served as a means to clarify amorphous fragments of memory, and sometimes helped contain waves of stored up emotion.

Beyond my personal reveries, I chose to write in a general way about the circumstances of young women who lost babies in the closed adoption system prevalent in the United States in the 1950s and 1960s. This is not because I presume that my recollections and feelings are wholly representative but because I believe there are many parallels in our stories. I had hoped to create a bit more understanding for those spouses, partners, children and friends of this particular segment of birth mothers, and to speak as well to interested adoptees and adoptive parents. Obviously, the personal opinions I express about various aspects of adoption are completely my own.

I also wanted to share my thoughts with colleagues. Therapists may believe they do not do "post adoption work" if they are not among the professionals who specialize in the field of adoption. But, as Waldron observes:

> "There are approximately 6 million adoptees in the United States. By extension, there are 12 million birth parents and 12 million adoptive parents - 30 million people directly involved in adoption. Add to that the untraceable millions of other birth and adoptive relations, and the percentage of our population touched by the act of adoption grows beyond imagination.

In the nineties, there will be record numbers of birth relations looking for each other. The babies born during the peak years of U.S. adoptions - 1969 and 1970 - have reached their young twenties, and they are searching now."[1]

Stiffler points out:

"For many separated persons, an unspoken, deep need for reunion pervades their lives. There is an urgent demand for clinical services to catch up to this reality."[2]

Few undergraduate or graduate psychology programs focus on the specific dynamics of adoption. There are, for those interested in the topic, a number of books that address the needs and concerns of adoptees and adoptive parents. Fewer resources exist for the mental health professional who sits with a woman who relinquished a child for adoption. I had written my doctoral dissertation on the long-term effects of surrender on a cohort of birth mothers. The responses I received from the women who participated in my study confirmed over and over what the literature on relinquishment shows: long-term chronic grief and diminished self esteem following loss of the infant. The lack of informed choice and inattention by mental health professionals to their needs during pregnancy were directly related to the sadness and rage that lingered, sometimes for decades.[3]

This is not news to the legions of women involved in search and support groups and/or adoption reform. I do think it is unfamiliar information to a majority of mental health workers and other helping professionals. I hope that at least some of what is recorded here is received with openness so that birth mothers who seek help will find receptive listeners.

GHOST MOTHER

"**W**hat, exactly, is a birth mother?" My colleague's puzzled look reminded me that to those unfamiliar with the world of adoption, including mental health professionals, it may mean nothing at all. The term may evoke in movie and television fans a stereotype: drug addicted woman unfit to parent, addled air head, teenager, prostitute, psychopath.

Generally speaking, a birth mother is simply a woman who has lost a child to adoption. There is a particular subset of women in this population about whom relatively little is written. These were not abusive or neglectful mothers, but rather girls who had become pregnant out of wedlock and who were made to pay the ultimate price: the loss of their babies.

Everyone has pain. There is not much humanity in comparing degrees of pain; the human condition is so rife with tragedy that comparisons are odious. Debates over which group of people have suffered more than another, or what kind of loss is worse than another hold no meaning for me. But, I do believe some of the most difficult losses are those that the griever, for one reason or another, keeps to himself or herself. The term "disenfranchised grief" has been used to describe such unacknowledged, incomplete mourning which casts the bereaved into a state of disjunction and disconnection - a sense of being alone in the world, cut off from support and understanding.[1] In the world of adoption, keen pain has been experienced by infertile couples, adoptees, and birth parents. I believe least is written about birth parents, and that birth mothers are arguably the most vulnerable of the triad to disenfranchisement in their

4

grief.

My story is similar to those of millions of women who relinquished infants for adoption in a specific moment in this country's history. Still "in the closet", countless middle aged women hide the fact of a firstborn child, relinquished to strangers to raise as their own.

The existential loss of self is endemic among birth mothers, especially those who have given up babies in a secret system where the relinquishing mother has become a ghost-like presence: an invisible fantasy figure existing at the edges of consciousness in the adoptee and adoptive parents.

In her book *Journey of the Adopted Self*, Lifton alludes to the psychic world of all triad members in the closed adoption system and the secret psychological spaces inhabited by its members in what she calls the Ghost Kingdom. Lifton says:

> "Unless one is aware of these ghosts, one will never be able to understand or to help the child who is adopted, the parents who adopt, or the parents who give up a child to adoption.
>
> The adopted child is always accompanied by a ghost of the child he might have been had he stayed with his birth mother and by the ghost of the fantasy child his adoptive parents might have had. He is also accompanied by the ghost of the birth mother, from whom he has never completely disconnected, and the ghost of the birth father, hidden behind her.
>
> The adoptive mother and father are accompanied by the ghost of the perfect biological child they might have had, who walks beside the adopted

child who is taking its place.

The birth mother (and father, to a lesser extent) is accompanied by a retinue of ghosts. The ghost of the baby she gave up, the ghost of her lover whom she connects with the baby, the ghost of the mother she might have been, and the ghosts of the baby's adoptive parents."[2]

❀

SEPARATION OF MOTHERS AND BABIES AS SOCIAL POLICY

Researchers have examined the emotional and psychological aftermath of losing an infant to closed, secret adoption.[1] Unlike the mother who loses a child through induced abortion, natural abortion (miscarriage) or infant death, the surrendering mother knows her child is alive and this critical difference impedes her ability to complete mourning and eventually accept the loss of the child. Millen and Roll discuss the "pathological bereavement" of the birth mother and explain how it is different from other maternal losses:

> "To come to terms with the loss, the individual must accept the loss as permanent. The yearning and searching impulses in the grief reaction must be recognized as expressions of longing but cannot be used to deny the finality of the loss."[2] However, for the surrendering mother, the child still exists. Millen and Roll note that searching is an expected element in a natural grief reaction. The bereaved may scan a crowd hoping to see the lost person. But for mothers who have surrendered their infants:

> "The urge to search is complicated...since their searching impulses are not irrational, and further may not be futile. Unlike the grieving person who eventually comes to terms with the fact that the lost person is truly dead, these mothers know that their child is alive and that the possibility of future contact may be more than a fantasy."[3]

Other factors distinguish the loss of a child to relinquishment in a closed adoption. Unlike the mother who suffers a loss through death or miscarriage for whom there is emotional support, the relinquishing mother is blamed by society and herself for "giving away" her child. She is viewed as rejecting and even abnormal. The data comparing long-term effects on women who opt for abortion versus relinquishment is not clear or consistent. The abortion experience is similar in that there are no mourning rituals in place for the loss. Abortion, however, does have a finality that does not exist for the relinquishing mother. It has been noted in the literature that the issue of manipulation and coercion is significant in terms of long-term effects of abortion. Like the relinquishing mother, the woman who aborts her fetus seems to suffer great conflict if she perceives that the decision was forced upon her with little or no exploration of the ramifications of her choice.[4,5]

Only a few decades ago unmarried white mothers were encouraged to give babies up for adoption largely because they were single. Rickie Solinger's research on single pregnancy and race before Roe v. Wade offers a disturbing yet engrossing analysis of the treatment of unmarried women who became pregnant following World War II.[6] Solinger has documented the shifts in cultural mores and social policies in that era which led to what she terms the "adoption mandate" - a philosophy that promoted relinquishment of so called illegitimate white babies. She notes that prior to World War II both white and black unwed mothers were expected to keep their babies, albeit as stigmatized mothers. The original policies and practices of maternity homes which housed unmarried pregnant mothers were based on the expectation that mothers and babies would remain together. It was not until the adoption mandate that separation of mother and baby would become policy.

A number of conditions following the second World War led to the mandate that white unmarried mothers give up their babies for adoption. More females were having sexual relations outside of marriage. The lack of effective birth control and legal abortion resulted in larger numbers of babies being born to unmarried mothers. Postwar glorification of the nuclear family created a context in which infertile married couples were encouraged to adopt infants. Black infants were not highly sought after by white couples who might wish to adopt. Further, the African American community unlike the white community, has traditionally found resources and a commitment within the extended family to care for infants born to unwed mothers. Solinger points out:

> "Social workers and other human service professionals claimed repeatedly that black single pregnancy was the product of family and community disorganization. Yet in comparing the responses among blacks and whites to an out of wedlock pregnancy and child bearing, it is striking how the black community organized itself to accommodate mother and child, while the white community was totally unwilling and unable to do so. The white community simply organized itself to expel them."[7]

Solinger's assertion that the black family generally accommodated to include the mother and baby, in contrast to the white community's expulsion of the unwed mother, is supported by other historians and social analysts.[8,9,10,11]

Coontz notes that the experience of black families has been "qualitatively different from that of whites, or even other minorities, all along the line, creating distinct family and gender traditions."[12] Under slavery, new family relations were improvised and slave families also drew on "African traditions of child fosterage and extended lineage lines...Grandmothers played a more central role in child rearing than they did in most white families, and slaves built a generalized kinship system in which all adults looked after the children."[13] She also states that "After the Civil War, African Americans went to tremendous lengths to track down kin, reunite families, and resist destabilizing family conditions, such as gang labor."[14]

In her study of kinship issues and adoption, Wegar says that the "relative informality of adoption in African American communities has been explained by the greater flexibility of kinship terms and obligations in these communities."[15] McGoldrick also notes "People of African descent place great importance on the family. In Africa, close-knit families and kinship groups were the foundations of the larger social structure of the tribe and the nation. Although slavery scattered families...it could not destroy their desire to reconstitute themselves...Living with the constant threat of separation and loss through the sale of a family member by a white master, the family sustained itself by placing high value on each member, no matter how distant the blood relationship may be...It is not unusual to find a child of a distant relative living in a home as part of a family...It is expected that members of the family will provide assistance to each other in times of crisis."[16]

However, even young black women who may have considered relinquishment were not afforded the same services as white unmarried mothers due to the racial segregation practiced in the United States at that time. Most maternity homes were closed to African Americans, who were expected to keep their babies (and were then scapegoated for doing so.) Race specific policies and practices had emerged during the depression years that served to punish the black unwed mother. In a curious twist, and an example of the differential way society punished black and white unmarried mothers, black mothers who did explore the idea of relinquishment were considered criminally neglectful. Solinger cites a 1950s case in which a black mother who tried to put her baby up for adoption was charged with desertion.[17]

At the same time, new psychological theories had developed that redefined the meaning of out of wedlock pregnancy among white unmarried mothers.

During the 1940s, mental health professionals shifted from a position which viewed the unmarried white mother as intellectually deficient or immoral (whose infant would also be stigmatized as genetically tainted) to the view that she was psychologically maladjusted. Unmarried pregnancy among white girls thus became a psychological problem amenable to rehabilitation. Casework services developed which were designed to promote rehabilitation through relinquishment of the baby to a waiting, married couple. Typical of mental health attitudes of the time, a social worker wrote in 1947 that "we know from psychiatric orientation and from casework experience that most unmarried pregnancy has a neurotic base."[18] This social worker, admitting that in her view the wise decision on the unwed mother's part would be to relinquish the child for adoption, explained her role in helping "Miss A":

> "The worker helped Miss A to see that she was using the baby as a symbol of neurotic need and that she did not have to keep it on that basis. The worker also evaluated Miss A's ability to support and rear a child in a community that would not accept illegitimacy. She took responsibility for helping the client to know that her contribution as a mother would be to relinquish the child. Although Miss A wavered at times, the caseworker consistently pointed out Miss A was doing the best thing for herself and the child. Following placement of the baby, Miss A successfully completed a course in beauty culture."[19]

With the problem of white illegitimacy redefined as psychological rather than genetic the baby became a valued commodity for waiting couples. The "relinquishment culture" of the maternity home helped many girls make the decision to give up their babies and by the late 1950s over 95% of these unmarried mothers surrendered their infants.[20] Social workers believed that only the most profoundly disturbed girls would insist on keeping and raising their babies. One of the foremost authorities in the field of social welfare at that time declared: "The caseworker has to clarify for herself the differences between the feelings of the normal (married) woman for her baby and the fantasy use of the child by the neurotic, unmarried mother."[21]

"Rehabilitation" was not possible for the black unwed mother. Redemption through relinquishment was possible only for the white mother who was counseled to surrender her baby and resume life unscathed by scandal. Virtually no attention was given to the possibility that she might forever grieve over her lost child.

Secrecy in infant adoption was reinforced via the creation in the 1930s and 1940s of the "sealed adoption record." Up until this time adoption records were not sealed but were available to adoptees. By the end of the 1940s most states had, for the first time, initiated laws that sealed records identifying the birth parents and the "illegitimate" label given the baby. Upon adoption, a brand new birth certificate with the names of the adoptive parents would be issued, erasing from memory the identity of the biological parents. In the 1950s, adoptee activist groups began forming and challenging the constitutionality of disallowing original records to adult adoptees. The issue of opening up records to give adoptees identifying information regarding birth parents is still being argued. At this time the only states that allow adult adoptees access to their original birth records are Alabama, Alaska, Delaware, Hawaii, Kansas,

Tennessee, and Oregon.

Mantecon[22] has proposed a triple bind theory to illustrate the dilemma that has been faced by the mother who relinquished her baby. Labeled a "bad girl" for becoming pregnant, she experienced shame, guilt, and fear. Those to whom she went for help counseled relinquishment as the only responsible decision, a loving sacrifice that would be in the best interest of the child and herself. Upon relinquishment, however, she would be warned never to speak of her shameful experience. Further, she would hear shocked references by acquaintances and in the media to the rejecting, uncaring woman who gives away her own flesh and blood. Society's opprobrium ensured her silence. Chesler has reminded us that "It is important to remember that when a birth mother does give her baby up for altruistic reasons, she is still reviled, feared, hated and unendingly punished."[23]

Adoption is an enormous, complex topic. There are many different kinds of adoption: infant adoption (closed or open); transracial adoption; international adoption; adoption that follows termination of parental rights due to child abuse or neglect. This book is primarily concerned with what happened to young women who became pregnant in a certain time and place: prior to abortion, effective (or even legal) birth control, social acceptance of either premarital sex or single parenting, and in a culture that promoted relinquishment of infants without any notion of the long-term emotional consequences either for the infant or for the mother who gave birth.

❁

A WINDOW OF TIME

"**Y**ou are a minor. Given your age, I will have to tell your parents, unless you do."

I had been throwing up for weeks and I knew I was pregnant. I was terrified, virtually immobilized, frozen with guilt and fear. I'd have fled on a Greyhound bus to anywhere far away if I'd not been so violently ill, vomiting every day until I retched bile. My step-mother made the medical appointment for me, as always, because at nineteen I was still perceived as a little girl in my family.

My first-ever pelvic exam ended with the doctor asking me, incredulously, "Is it at all possible that you are *PREGNANT?*" Out of my childlike magical thinking I had dared imagine I might escape detection. Perhaps the doctor could be fooled into thinking I'd contracted some sort of exotic virus. But reality could no longer be denied: my parents would be told unless I confessed first.

I have thought back occasionally to the physician's statement and it strikes me as odd, at least in our present day and age, that I was pronounced a 'minor' at the age of nineteen. This snapshot in my mind highlights the differences between 1963 and today's world in which pregnant adolescents have more of an ability to obtain mental health and medical services independently. I never questioned the physician's obligation to tell my parents I was pregnant even though I desperately wanted the information to remain confidential.

Birth mothers who have written about relinquishment have noted the staggering social changes within only a few decades. Lynn Franklin recalls:

"The social stigma of our situation was considered untenable, and our parents assumed authority over us. We were for the most part quite young and often emotionally immature, and without financial resources we acquiesced and did what we were told."[1]

Patricia E. Taylor gets it exactly right when she says:

"The most important thing to remember about 1961 is that it was not really in the sixties. 1961 was firmly embedded in the rules, mores and values of the fifties and before. Women were allowed to further their education, but their ultimate goal was to achieve the title of "Mrs." Men were to work to support their families; women stayed home to take care of those families. If a woman worked, she was taking that job from a man. Women were not even supposed to call men on the phone. They were expected to sit home and wait to be called. Women who were daring enough to call men were considered aggressive. Women who were "pregnant too soon" were "in trouble."[2] I would add that pregnant girls were expelled from school and pregnant women could be refused employment.

Jane O'Reilly remembers that "In 1958, an out-of-wedlock pregnancy was literally disgraceful (so limited was the range of behavior for a middle class girl.) Ironically, my generation's revolution was so successful in expanding those limits that now my children cannot begin to understand what it was like."[3]

The relinquishment culture of the 1950s and 1960s brings to mind the observation of Clarissa Pinkola Estes who has written:

> "When a mother is forced to choose between the child and the culture, there is something abhorrently cruel and unconsidered about the culture. A culture that requires harm to one's soul in order to follow the culture's proscription is a very sick culture indeed. This 'culture' can be the one a woman lives in, but more damning yet, it can be the one she carries around and complies with in her own mind."[4]

INTERLUDE

I don't recall how it was that a neighbor caught a glimpse of me in my fifth month of pregnancy, just prior to entering the board and wage home where my 'condition' would be observed only by complete strangers. I had quit my clerical job at an insurance company with a feigned excuse about a family crisis in another state and had remained hidden for the most part in my parents' apartment. In any event, a woman whom I had known casually from the building greeted me and invited me to her unit to look over some maternity clothes she was willing to share. Inarticulate and unassertive I accepted the clothing passively and fearfully. How would I explain to my parents the acquisition of this wardrobe? My step-mother had coached me to tell anyone who asked about my absent "husband" - a story which as I recall had to do with his being away in the Navy. I remember wearing a cheap wedding band. I returned home laden with maternity blouses and skirts, furtive and quiet but unable to sneak into my room undetected. My step-mother furiously demanded to know where the clothing had come from. In a rage that the secret might be revealed, and that I had talked to someone and accepted a few minutes of kindness, she ordered me to return everything. I gathered the clothing up, knocked on the neighbor's door, stammered an apology and left. I still see the sad and bewildered look on her face as she moved to close the door behind me.

DECISION OR DIRECTIVE?

The Florence Crittenden Home for Unwed Mothers was packed to capacity. There would be no openings until I was seven months pregnant. In the interim, in order to hide me from even my relatives, who were unaware of my pregnancy, the maternity home arranged for me to live with a family in suburban Virginia where I would be given room and board plus a wage of $20 a week in return for child care and light housekeeping duties. The salary would enable me to pay for the services of the home.

I arrived at the wage home in January 1964. It was a comfortable dwelling in a quiet upper middle class neighborhood. I shared a room with "Nancy", a girl my age who was further along in her pregnancy and therefore preparing to enter the Crittenden Home in a few weeks. She introduced me to my chores and responsibilities. The 'lady of the house' was in the hospital giving birth to her fifth child the day I arrived.

Housekeeping, cooking and babysitting kept me occupied during the day. It was in the early morning and later at night that feelings of isolation, fear and near panic would erupt, my mind racing. I prayed constantly to slow down the thoughts and images. Fantasies of keeping my baby also provided comfort until I allowed myself to assess the reality of my situation: I hadn't heard from the baby's father in months; there would be no emotional or financial support from my horrified and scandalized parents. I considered the prospect of ekeing out a living as a clerk or typist while my baby was watched by strangers, as I knew no one personally who could help. I was flooded with guilt at bringing a life into the world under these circumstances as well as the knowledge that I had betrayed my own childhood dream of being a devoted mother to well cared for and happy children in a traditional family, unlike the sad, alcoholic home of my parents. For months, every person in whom I confided echoed the reaction of the birth father: "You'll give the baby up for adoption."

Yet doubt lingered. I discussed my reservations with Nancy. "How can a person give up her baby?" "Wouldn't a child feel rejected by the biological mother?" Nancy was firm and unequivocal in her response - that she was relinquishing because this was the best possible thing to do for the child's life.

I rode the bus into the city on days off. I imagined being rescued by a man who would fall madly in love with me and thus smitten would insist on marriage and helping me raise the baby. I daydreamed and wandered through the baby apparel sections of department stores, certain that the pretend wedding band on my left ring finger would fool observers into believing I was a properly married young woman. Back and forth: the reality, the fantasy, the reality. Eventually I faced the facts. No one would rescue me; no one would magically change my circumstances and help me create a stable, loving home for this child; there was no network of caring people to help us do more than barely survive. My vision of the future looked like a recreation of the lonely life I'd had as a child. I pictured a grim and stigmatized existence for the two of us.

By my sixth month I had internalized the mantra chanted by the social workers, my roommate Nancy, and it appeared, the larger society: "The only loving and responsible decision for an unwed girl with no resources is to relinquish the baby for adoption to people who can provide a stable home and far better life than you can give." I had internalized this so well that I repeated it to myself (and sometimes others) for decades after surrendering my baby.

But when is a decision not a decision?

I think that a genuine decision involves exploration of all options and the consequences of each. It also includes having knowledge of, and access to, resources. In 1964 the options for the typical white middle class girl were limited to either marriage or relinquishment. Once an adoptive home was found, even the former possibility appeared to threaten the system held neatly in place by counseling that served as a directive to put the child up for adoption.

Late in my pregnancy I contacted my baby's father and he came to visit me in the maternity home. The social worker was not pleased when I mentioned to her that my dim expectations of a future with him were looking more like a possibility. This social worker, generally an affable and pleasant woman, cast me an angry look and rising in her chair loudly asserted: "Not with this baby you won't! If you want to be with him and have another child go ahead, but you won't be with him and *THIS* child!"

When I look back, my anger is not around the issue of whether or not I was prevented from being with this boy because even then I really knew we had no future together. It just would have been nice to have been a participant in an honest discussion of all possible plans including marriage or single parenthood with all of the pros and cons. It is difficult to look back upon the 'counseling' offered and not rather harshly conclude that the birth mother was considered a breeder, with her baby a commodity for worthier people.

(As a postscript, I should note that shortly prior to delivering her baby, my wage home roommate, Nancy, who had steadfastly maintained her intention to relinquish, met a man, got married, and took her baby back to her home in another state. I was surprised at how betrayed I felt.)

DOING TIME

"**W**hen an unwed mother arrived on the doorstep, she came to join a society of mostly young women, all in a similar predicament. They were all subject to social stigma; they had caused their parents extreme difficulty; and most had been rejected by the boys or men with whom they'd had sex. The shared stigma was powerful. Many unwed mothers felt they had been removed from society and sent to homes during their pregnancies because their parents, their schoolmates and friends--the community in general--viewed them as criminals, or slightly more gently, as patients. It was difficult for an unwed mother to escape internalizing the notion that she was some sort of felon, incarcerated for committing an act of aggression against society."[1]

I hear that some birth mothers are trying to re-connect over the Internet with peers from their old maternity homes. I find this interesting and I assume that for many women it is part of putting the pieces of a life back together, akin to writing for hospital records (birth mothers are entitled to their own records, not their baby's) or contacting the adoption agency to give or receive information. I personally made no attachments in the Florence Crittenden Home for Unwed Mothers, where anonymity was expected; we were not allowed to use last names, only initials. For some birth mothers, the maternity home was a haven, a safe place. For others like myself it was de facto incarceration.

Days and nights have never again moved so slowly. My most vivid recollection of this institution was the television room. Every day I would sit with the other pregnant girls and contemplate the calendar on the wall adjacent to the t.v. Each month had some sort of theme or icon; days were crossed off as we stared at the calendar, each of us anticipating our due date, marking time.

It is sharply painful to think back to my first pregnancy with its overall quality of wonder and simultaneous sadness. Feeling my baby kick, I would smile and pat my tummy, then remember that this was baby was not mine. Understanding that I was becoming a mother, infused with awe at the idea of a new life developing inside me - but a life I would be no part of after giving birth. I had bought into the edict that punishment was appropriate for the crime of having gotten pregnant. I believed that the sacrifice of giving up my baby was only right, given what my parents and the larger society said about my sinful behavior. The anger I began to experience years later in "recovery" was linked to my growing understanding that becoming pregnant was not a crime against society. It is sobering to realize that I believed the surrender of my baby to better people was some sort of atonement. Today the notion seems insane.

❋

BIRTH DAY

It was a sweltering hot, sticky-humid, summer morning in Washington, D.C. I had paced all night long, the persistent ache in my lower back and tightening in my abdomen signaling the onset of labor, or so I figured. It was three days before my due date. I stopped pacing to quietly enter the room I shared with another girl, and pack a small suitcase for the hospital. I returned to the darkened hallways, walking back and forth until daybreak. My heart raced. I was not entirely sure I was in labor but as it had been at least seven hours since I'd first noticed the pain, and the tightness felt more and more pressured, I decided to find the nurse stationed on the floor beneath our dorm rooms. She instructed me to time my contractions and after ten minutes of lying in the sweaty morning bed, I asked to go to the hospital. A taxi was summoned and another staff person accompanied me to the hospital. As the contractions came closer and closer, my bag of water broke flooding the taxi cab floor. Both the driver and staff person seemed astonished, probably because I was very quiet on the ride, being a young person who viewed stoicism and enduring pain silently among the greatest of virtues.

I delivered quickly but not before I was anesthetized. I awakened with my head throbbing and a young doctor smiling and telling me I'd had a little girl. His visit was brief but very kind. I don't remember much more about my overnight stay in the hospital. I recall more clearly the early morning ride back to the maternity home, my baby placed by a volunteer in the car beside me. I gazed at this tiny sleeping infant whom I longed to hold. We rode back to the home where she was placed with the other babies in a nursery and I returned to a dorm room for girls who had delivered. In five days she would begin her life with her adoptive family, and in another week I would return to my parents' home expected to act as if nothing significant had occurred in my life. There would be no mourning ritual, no cards offering sympathy for my loss, no warm embrace or soft words of comfort.

LIFE GOES ON

Within two years of relinquishing my daughter I had moved to California, married, and given birth again. The literature on birth mothers shows that about half of us had gone on to bear several subsequent children, and about half of us never had another baby. There is a high unexplained secondary infertility rate among birth mothers which means that although many mothers chose not to have more children, quite often out of guilt, or loyalty to the first child, other women who wanted another child never conceived again for reasons that are not explained medically. This makes all the more poignant and tragic the easy assurances of social workers who advised that after the first baby was adopted by people more suitable for parenting, we would go on to have as many other children as we wanted when the time was right.

My son Larry's birth awakened a brightness in my spirit that had become dulled and almost devoid of joy. He was born in June, the same month as my firstborn. Although I had certainly not begun to deal with issues around the loss of my first child, or anything else significant in my life that had preceded my first pregnancy, I remember feeling very happy when our little boy was born and having the sense that my life was moving forward. At least I wouldn't have to hear any more advice about pregnancy and birth from acquaintances who had assumed this was my first pregnancy. Part of the "birth mother experience" is the tension around what to say when asked how many children you have, a jarring reminder of the baby you left behind, the child who exists but out of your knowing.

Larry died when he was almost six weeks old. The doctors told his father and me that our baby had died of unexplained causes - "crib death" they called it back then. I remember the funeral, Larry's tiny coffin covered with flowers, his father and I called to the pulpit to read. I remember crying an entire night and then shutting down emotionally for a long time. I have a hazy recollection of supportive ritual: cards, letters, a gathering after the memorial service to talk. Tears would not come again for many years, only confusion and anger that my first two children would be lost to me forever, when all I wanted was to give and receive love. One night shortly after I was reunited with my daughter, over two decades later, I had a dream in which Larry appeared. Except now he was older, and like his big sister, had just been somewhere else all that time, growing into an adult, and happy to see me.

❉

TRIGGERS

I can attest to the principle of expressing grief as a healthier and more functional way of handling psychological pain than denying and repressing the emotional fallout of a broken heart. Layer upon layer of stuffed down emotion - shame, rage, sorrow, carefully hidden and re-packaged into a pleasing, but artificial, public persona. Of course, if a birth mother grew up in a family with secrets and closed communication she is already conditioned to develop and maintain a false self; the pretense is as natural as breathing. This subterfuge is not without great cost. As life goes on after pregnancy, labor, and surrender of the infant, reminders of the unacknowledged loss tend to collide with unexpressed feelings swimming in a subterranean world. Birth mothers can tell you about triggers that push the pain to awareness. Just a few of the more common triggers include invitations to baby showers, the sight of other mothers together with their babies (even after birthing subsequent children), the anniversary of the lost child's birthday, songs that were popular at the time of pregnancy and relinquishment, the innocent and deadly question "How many children do you have"?

Even now, after reunion with my daughter and a good deal of healing, all of these triggers, and more, sometimes serve to overwhelm my emotional equilibrium. In these instances I silently experience an internal tumult of raging and wailing that, if visible, would undoubtedly startle a casual observer. But as a rule, I maintain my calm and impassive outer mask.

Relinquishment impacts the mother's sexual, spiritual and emotional "selves." Teller has discussed the "veil of shame" worn by birth mothers. She points out the need to undo the connection of sex with trauma, grief or shame.[1]

27

Mental health literature does not often, if ever, link Post Traumatic Stress Disorder and the mother who has relinquished an infant for adoption. The only references I have seen linking the two are in the literature specific to adoption.[2] Yet it is clear that there are a constellation of symptoms commonly seen in birth mothers which fit the criteria for PTSD. Some of these include:

Recurrent and intrusive distressing recollections of the event, including images, thoughts or perceptions; efforts to avoid thoughts, feelings or conversations associated with the trauma; efforts to avoid activities, places or people that arouse recollections of the trauma; inability to recall an important aspect of the trauma; feelings of detachment or estrangement from others; restricted range of affect.[3]

When Jones interviewed birth mothers for her book *Birth Mothers: Stories of Women Who Relinquished Children for Adoption*, she noted that some of these symptoms occurred with such regularity that they seemed to comprise a syndrome. The women she interviewed spoke of unresolved grief, symptoms of Post Traumatic Stress Disorder such as flashbacks, nightmares, anxiety, avoidance or phobic reactions. There was a sense of being 'stuck' ever since the relinquishment; unexplained secondary infertility; living in extremes (such as too controlling or too passive, having no other children or having a succession of subsequent children) and "dual identities" - what some might call a false outer self which masquerades to protect the vulnerable, isolated, shamed inner self.[4]

Although the secrecy of closed adoptions was cited by many of the mothers in Jones' study as creating the problems in adjustment, Jones noted that mothers who had relinquished in open adoption had many of the same difficulties.

❀

FINDING HER

Returning home from work late one evening, I find the house empty because my husband is out of town and the kids aren't home. The answering machine blinks and I press the message dial. Absent mindedly picking up a pen and foraging for a piece of paper in order to jot down messages, I suddenly freeze. "This is International Soundex calling. You may remember that you registered with us. Please call." My God, could it be? Of course I remember I had registered with Soundex, years ago, wanting to make it as easy as possible for her to find me, should she so desire. International Soundex is a free reunion registry in which adult adoptees and birth parents send whatever identifying information they have in the hopes a match can be found. I knew reunions happened to other people, but could I dare to hope that I could be so blessed? Alone in the house I pace, as I'd paced the night before giving birth twenty six years earlier: trembling, heart racing. I call Soundex but it is too late at night; their office closed. Talking to myself: "Relax, it may be nothing." My husband calls and hears the frantic hope in my voice. "Well, they may just be updating their records", he cautions. He knows what this means to me and wants to protect me from devastating disappointment. I am up all night, thinking, weeping, yet exhilarated. I eventually slide into bed, reading and re-reading the notebook I'd begun the day I knew I would need to try and find her. I read letters I had written to the adoption agency, records I had gotten from the hospital, the social study I'd received about the adoptive parents, random musings that I had recorded. I'm up at dawn, manic, unable to be still any longer. Too early to telephone, I scrub the kitchen floor, then resume pacing. I call Soundex. I'm put through to its director, Tony Vilardi. After asking me a few questions he confirms that there appears to be a match, but he'll call me right back. Within minutes he calls and says there is a very excited young lady in West Virginia who will welcome my call from California. He gives me her name and telephone number adding that I'm a grandmother because she just had a baby of her own. Twenty six years later I'm talking to my first child, now a mother herself.

Within two months we were sitting close to each other on a sofa in her cozy trailer while her baby slept. My daughter has been a writer and poet from childhood and she'd kept diaries, journals, pictures and poems which she shared with me.

In the neat penmanship of a young girl, a letter on three ring binder paper caught my heart:

Dear Mom,

I know this is hard for you, maybe more than it is for me. I'm sorry if it hurts you, but I had to find you. You don't know what it's like growing up and wondering where your mom is, wondering if she ever thinks of you, or even cares at all. It's hard knowing your mother's out there somewhere, and you can't see her, talk to her, or be a part of her at all even though you're her first born daughter. But then you think, but she didn't want me, she rejected me, gave me away. I'm sorry, but I've caught up with you. Please, just let me talk to you. I hope I haven't wrecked your life.

Love, your forgotten daughter

And another letter, written only months earlier, during her pregnancy:

To my mom,

Once again I need to write to you. Thoughts of you come in waves - times you're on my mind and I can't think of anything else, and times when you rest in the back of my subconscious - but you're always there. This mysterious extension of myself that I'm not allowed to know, see, touch, or hug.

I've had good parents, they've loved me a lot but people don't understand why I need to know you. "The past is the past" they say. It makes me furious! This is my damn life! Not theirs! I refuse to take any more of their guilt trips -- it's my life and feelings. They have no power to take that away from me anymore.

I miss you even though I don't know you. There have been times in my life when I have really needed you though. No one else could be there for me and I've felt so alone - I just knew if you were here you'd hug me and tell me everything will be okay. It's like I've always felt out of place in my family - like I should have been somewhere else. I was just different. I thought differently, I don't know, it's all so confusing.

Where are you? Do you think about me? Do you want to know me? Talk to me? Are you happy? Do you have other children? I hope you haven't forgotten me - I always think about you on my birthday and thank you for having me.

I haven't minded being adopted, sometimes it makes me feel special. But other times it makes me feel sad.

I'm going to be having a baby in a few months. What will she look like? It's so hard to imagine having someone who looks like me, who is my own flesh and blood. How people take that for granted - and it's so important to me! It's SO important. I get so made at other people I just want to scream and say...

Oh I don't know. I'm tired of feeling angry. I'm just tired right now.

This little baby kicks me all the time now, reminding me that he (or she) is there, telling me everything will be okay. I get a lot of strength from this child. I wonder how you felt being pregnant with me. Did you talk to me? Want me? Care about me? I wonder if I look like you or my father. Did you like him? Was he nice? Did he know about me? I'm not mad at you, I really feel you cared about me. I don't know, maybe I felt it when I was still in the womb, I believe that.

Oh, I must find you, see you, talk to you, touch you. It would make me so happy.

There's an empty place in my soul where I miss you. I have no conscious memories of you but you're such a big part of my life, it's strange.

I believe that before I was born and still in the spirit world that I chose this experience to go thru, that I chose you to be the woman to give birth to me, and chose my parents to raise me. I don't believe in accidents. For some reason this was meant to be, I suppose. I just hope that somewhere in the great Plan of Life that we are destined to meet in this lifetime. I think we are! I feel it in my heart and I will never give up.

Wherever you are, I'm thinking about you and wanting to know you.

Can you hear me.......!

Your daughter of long ago

BIRTH MOTHER AS WIMP

I was surprised to discover, once I began to read and listen to the stories of other birth mothers, that many women felt shamed not only about expressing their sexuality as teenagers, which had led to tragic consequences, but also of their perceived weakness at not keeping and raising their babies.

I do not remember feeling weak for having relinquished my baby. Sad, "bad", conflicted - yes. Not weak. It is true that I did not have sufficient information at that time to make a fully informed decision given the philosophy of social work practice in that era coupled with no family support. Few of us did have the kind of guidance and support we needed. But given the information I did have, I came to believe in the wisdom of relinquishment and groomed myself to let go of my baby after birth. However flawed the decision or the process of reaching it, I did sign relinquishments papers, and watched as the adoptive parents' social worker carried my baby away to begin her life with them when she was five days old. I remember feeling that I would never be the same and that I had sacrificed part of my very being. I also remember that I felt strong for being able to do what I thought was the right thing for my child. Decades later, armed with more information, it is easy to rethink the whole matter. But at that time I did my best and I did it virtually on my own. That took guts. I was shocked later in life to be patronized by a support group leader who figuratively patted me on the head saying "you poor thing, you just didn't know your rights." Well, there may be some truth to that but I resented being thought of as a "poor thing."

In his excellent book on open adoption, James Gritter offers an interesting comparison of relinquishment as based in either shame (the mother did not care enough about her baby; was forced/tricked into relinquishment; was unsupported, gave up too easily; was paralyzed by fear; took the easy path) or honor (it was sensible; grounded in love; a moral conviction; self sacrificing; responsible).[1] I think many of us in the closed, secret system relinquished from a combination of shame and honor. It should not be forgotten that whether or not an unwed pregnant mother in that era felt she made a genuine choice or not, she acted in a historical context that set the tone. It is disconcerting to realize that desiring to keep and raise one's baby as an "unwed mother" (no one used the term "single parent" in those days) was prima facie evidence of mental illness, or at least neurosis. Solinger's research shows us that the years from 1945 until Roe v. Wade were one historical moment in which giving up so-called "illegitimate" white babies was encouraged. Shame was built right into the institution of closed secret adoption. We pregnant girls knew that "decent" people held us in contempt. So some birth mothers may feel they were weak, stupid or worse. Others accept that they made the best decision they could. Still other women look back on their younger selves and conclude that they were loving, wise, brave. We may vacillate between all of these judgments of ourselves at one time or another. I would argue, however, that it is time to debunk the stereotype of birth mother as wimp.

Memories and feelings are illusory; they pass from one form to another changing in size, shape, and content over time. But this is what I remember without a doubt: an inner determination that I would not let my baby be placed into foster care limbo while I tried to make up my mind what to do. I knew there had to be an immediate home for him or her. I knew I had to take good care of myself and prepare my unborn child and myself for separation by telling us both that other people waited who would love and care for him or her. In retrospect I wonder at my naive trust in authority figures who seemed to know what was best. But I have the luxury of a fully lived life in which to reassess how I handled my first pregnancy. I am beginning to understand that, in the

35

end, it is all right: that I did my best, out of both shame and honor.

CUTOFFS

Emotional cutoffs are estrangements that occur in families where there is minimal contact or no contact at all due to conflict, anger, hurt feelings. Family system therapists view cutoffs as emblematic of dysfunction because the fracturing of family relationships, when unhealed, can lead to problems through the generations. For example, a woman emotionally cut off from her mother may be vulnerable in the future as the relationship with her own daughter becomes overly needy and enmeshed or marked by hostility. Family therapists see that resolving the issues between family members in a clearer way breaks the unhealthy intergenerational transmission of interpersonal problems.

Closed adoption creates cutoffs. Whereas a working open adoption links kinship systems, closed adoption fractures kinship ties. Furthermore, where there are secrets, and where thoughts and feelings about her experience are submerged, the birth mother's healing is thwarted. A relinquishing mother is at risk of playing out her unresolved loss in future relationships. Research indicates that there is a tendency for her to overprotect future children. On the other hand, some birth mothers find it difficult to attach to subsequent children. As noted previously, a high percentage of birth mothers never have another child, often out of guilt, a sense that it would be a betrayal to the child she let go.

Reflect upon the multiplicity of cutoffs the relinquishing mother has experienced: cut off from family, friends, community, perhaps from the birth father. Most profoundly, cut off from the girl she had been, the woman she was becoming, cut off from her own needs, hopes, dreams.

Imagine the entrapment of the birth mother who has never

confided in her husband or subsequent children the birth of another child. How devastating to her soul to be so cut off from this life-changing experience: having conceived, carried and delivered a baby who has disappeared into another family to be parented. Nowadays it is considered good social work practice to talk with a mother considering relinquishment about her responsibility to her child by providing information, perhaps on an ongoing basis. As the child grows up he or she will benefit from open information. In the heydey of relinquishment, of course, the birth mother's usefulness was complete once she had delivered a healthy baby.

I remember my extreme trepidation about the prospect of telling my children about their older sister. Ultimately, the longing to find her and the need to stop keeping secrets overcame my shame and terror. Nancy Verrier, in her seminal book on adoptees, *The Primal Wound*, says that she believes guilt, not shame, is induced by relinquishment.[1] Verrier suggests that shame would have originated in her family of origin, not in the relinquishment of her baby. I am not so sure of this. It is no doubt true that many relinquishing mothers were raised in shame based families. But it seems to me that a disempowered pregnant girl could not remain unscathed in a system that promoted relinquishment around her perceived mental instability and incompetence to parent. Even a person who had felt reasonably good about herself before pregnancy, in this social climate would be vulnerable to the development of humiliation and shame.

In any event, the pervasive need to find my oldest child overcame my terror at the possible loss of my other children's respect. I had remarried in my late twenties; my husband knew about my loss and silent grief. His support greatly facilitated my telling our three children about my oldest daughter. I was enveloped in the sweetness of their loving response. I cannot know what it was really like for each of them, to hear that their mother had hidden the existence of another child, their sibling. I know for myself that opening to them in this way was a huge step forward in beginning to repair the emotional fractures of my life, and in our family history. When my youngest child was in college, years later, she wrote a series of poems for an English class that recalled from her point of view the events leading up to our reunion with her sister. I knew she understood the essence of my soul's cutoff when she wrote:

"After giving the baby up, she stopped laughing. The kind of laugh that comes from the inside was gone...When she started to search out the adult child, she started looking for that laugh again. Looking for the part of her that got left behind."

❀

THERAPY

By the time I entered therapy in my late 30s I had finally begun to grieve out loud. In the privacy of my counselor's office I revisited events and issues I'd become expert at internalizing, beginning with my mother's death when I was six years old and moving through other significant losses. When I was ready to talk about losing my baby to adoption it was the first time I'd cried for any length of time about this event. Many birth mothers, too overcome with shame or too shut down emotionally, do not see the connection between relinquishment and depression, relationship problems, or other difficulties.

Counselors who understand the context in which adoptions occurred years ago will know that the decision of whether or not to be single mother, which is taken for granted today, was "virtually unimaginable in the recent past."[1] It is interesting to note that the highest teenage birth rate ever recorded in the United States was in 1957. The incidence of illegitimacy was masked because the marriage age dropped sharply in this period and the adoption of white "illegitimate" babies was encouraged.[2,3,4]

Birth mothers were routinely advised that in time the relinquishment would be forgotten and life would resume normally. But as Roles has noted, "Living with the uncertainty of knowing how her child is faring has been identified by birth parents as the most difficult aspect of coping."[5] Mental health professionals were not aware of the long-term emotional consequences for their unmarried pregnant clients and tended to offer facile reassurances, disregarding the mother's need to grieve.

Brodzinski has outlined criteria of adaptive grieving. These include having a safe haven in which to mourn; freedom to express feelings and behave differently; proximity, empathy and warmth; rituals of passing, and opportunity for reorganization.[6] All of these criteria were compromised in the case of the relinquishing mother. Millen and Roll say "the counseling process must validate the reality of their loss and aid these women in their exploration of guilt and anger, both at themselves and those around them."[7]

The birth mothers who participated in my study overwhelmingly found individual therapy sought years after relinquishment a disappointing, ineffective or even hurtful exercise. One woman said:

> "At the therapist's office the ball was not picked up, i.e. no response really, no indication she "got" in any way the impact of adoption on a mother. I've received a variety of responses by other counselors most of which implied they simply did not 'get it' and know how to respond."[8]

Another woman cried as she told her counselor she had given up her first baby for adoption. "The counselor just gave me a blank stare. I never brought it up again."[9]

It is an enormous step for a woman to even bring up the topic of relinquishment in counseling. Active listening and conveying acceptance is critically important in order to establish a therapeutic alliance. Therapists who work with trauma cite the importance of "establishing safety, reconstructing the trauma story and restoring the connection between survivors and their community."[10] A blank stare, or other response that trivializes her experience interferes with the establishment of a safe environment. Trauma damages a person's ability to trust; many birth mothers are exquisitely sensitive to judgment and rejection.

The therapist is wise to treat the relinquishment experience with respect. Some birth mothers will deny the significance of their experience. Rather than pressuring her to "break" the denial, it would be beneficial to hear and honor her feelings, continuing to create a safe place. As is true with rape survivors or other trauma victims, it is necessary to respect the client's internal pace.

Remember that the needs of unmarried mothers, especially those who lost babies during the years of the 'adoption mandate' were considered irrelevant. Processing her experience offers the birth mother an opportunity to build a sense of agency and power. Years of silence may have kept her stuck developmentally. Basic self esteem strategies and recognition of her strengths are important.

A mother who expresses sorrow over the loss of her child must be validated because she was enjoined from mourning. In fact, her efforts to comply with directives to "forget" have often led her to suppress thoughts and feelings leading to vague, fragmented memories or even amnesia for certain aspects of the pregnancy and surrender. Mothers who begin to search may feel additional guilt when details, perhaps even the child's birth date, seem blurry or unclear. Therapists can help the mother understand that this is normal and not evidence that she didn't care enough to remember. Journaling is a helpful tool to help reconstruct the events around pregnancy and relinquishment.

In the face of chronic grief, including the low level of depression experienced by many birth mothers, it may be useful to consider the manner in which the sorrow of relinquishment can foster a deeper capacity to honor the pain in oneself and others. Writers and poets have spoken of the pain of a broken heart as a catalyst to such opening. Letting go of self judgment and blame of others is a process over time. Forgiveness of the younger self is a central task in healing. This younger self did the best she could in that personal and historical time and place. Absolution for the mother bereaved through adoption begins with a willingness to forgive herself.

It may take longer to let go of rage at the other players in the complex human drama of surrender: social workers, parents, birth fathers, clergy and others who were unwilling or unable to accommodate the idea that mother and baby were already forming a family and that to sever their bond would have life-long ramifications. I find that acceptance is a more reachable goal than "forgiveness" and that acceptance includes the understanding that those people had their own frailty, lack of knowledge, ignorance and fear. It is worth letting go, as best we can, of the bitterness that erodes one's spirit.

Search has been described as an effort to find one's lost self[11,12] and as a spiritual journey.[13] The process of the search can be curative. In returning to the past, remembering the thoughts and feelings during pregnancy, and moving past secrecy and shame the birth mother usually begins to think about whether or not searching will be part of her drive to integration and wholeness. Regrets may haunt one long after an event with regrets of inaction the most powerful.[14] Search may represent a stance against passivity and inaction which hinder the resolution of emotional pain. One does not necessarily "recover" from the loss of a child but restoration of positive self-esteem and a sense of personal agency follow taking action. It is important to help the client assess the meaning and significance of her search. What is the fantasy around finding? Exploration of expectations and envisioning all possible scenarios, including the possibility of rejection, is necessary.

The literature is clear that most reunions are welcomed, and often produce "elation, catharsis, and ecstacy"[15] but some separated persons (birth parent or adoptee) are not ready or even able emotionally to reconnect. Although this is the exception it can be a crushing blow if expectations are unrealistic. This is why preparation and support are crucial.

Whether or not the mother will attempt to reunite with her child lost to adoption, her long-term adjustment includes learning to live with the longing. She can never go back and parent her child as an infant, toddler, school-age child, and teenager. Mourning what has been lost and self examination is needed whether the mother decides to search or not. On one level, searching is about finding the other person. On a deeper level, it is a journey of mind, heart and soul which offers the opportunity to "reawaken what is already wise and strong"[16] within oneself.

THE HEALING WORKSHOP

The workshop was held in a cozy setting on a quiet sunny day. Our group consisted of six birth mothers with a licensed counselor as facilitator and a birth mother acting as co-facilitator. I had recently decided to initiate a search for my daughter, who was now a young adult, and was excited to be a member of a daylong "healing workshop for birth mothers."

I was curious about what the day would bring, slightly nervous, but very open about participating for the first time in a group setting with others who shared this life-altering experience. Although relinquishment was ubiquitous in the 1960s it is telling how rarely one uncovers another birth mom. The co-facilitator was warm. She listened, nodded, exuded acceptance. The official leader seemed aloof, distant. Nevertheless, I felt okay because this was an opportunity to process old, old pain in the company of people who would understand. I had been in individual therapy and had worked on my adoption loss to a point, but the group experience would be a new forum in which to continue the repair work on my bruised psyche. I also felt that I could contribute as well as receive.

After introductions and a few exercises in which we brainstormed and made lists of what we had lost, gained, learned through pregnancy and relinquishment, I relaxed. Group settings have been, and continue to be, difficult for me. My social anxiety can be debilitating if I allow it to gain control in group settings. Yet here, I knew that I was an expert on my own experience, and that there was no need to cover up, to pretend to feel happier, cheerier, more optimistic than I really felt because to put on these familiar masks would be to waste my time in a workshop designed to help us all "heal" from the trauma of surrender. When the leader asked for volunteers to role play I offered to participate. The scenario was a talk with my step-

45

mother about how I had felt when I disclosed my pregnancy, a what-I-had-needed-from-her type thing. The leader played the role of my step-mother. I spoke straight from my heart. I was hurt, I was angry. I had longed for love and reassurance but received cruel rejection not only of myself but my baby as well. The leader, cool, intellectual, disdainful, said she wanted to share how it felt from the step-mother point of view: blamed, judged too harshly. I was stunned. I remember thinking it was fortunate that this episode had not occurred years earlier, when I was emotionally more fragile. I withdrew mentally for the remainder of the day. My detached anger enabled me to see that I'd not been inappropriate - I was participating in a role-play situation set up by the trainer/leader. But I steadfastly refused to make myself vulnerable in any way during the remaining hours of the workshop.

Since that day in the early 1980s, I've encountered others who have a tendency to misuse their role as group or workshop leader/expert. In the guise of empowerment they disempower by talking for, talking over, and generally bossing around group members. There is at times, in this recovery work, a dogmatic certainty around how group members or listeners should feel, think, act. My adoptee friend, a gentle soul, is exhorted to become more militant in her search - to move faster, work harder! She cries on her way home from a support group meeting, embarrassed and distraught.

One year I traveled east to attend a national adoption conference. I was expecting my daughter to join me there for a few days and she was late arriving for the first workshop. I was nervous and edgy. I had expected to hear the presenter, listen to other participants and if moved to do so share some thoughts of my own. The longer I waited for my daughter to appear the more distracted and nervous I felt. Leaping to the conclusion that she wasn't going to show up at all, I held back tears. I began to think that she didn't want to meet me but had not told me, perhaps out of not wanting to disappoint me by saying so. The presenter insisted that everyone share their feelings. Allowing myself to be pressured to participate, I offered that as a birth mother, the greatest gift to me would be honesty in our relationship . I could hear my small, trembling words echo as if from a great distance. The workshop leader, who could in no way know that I'd spent nearly two decades reading, journaling, seeking out resources and in general "working on my issues" became adamant that I find a support group when I got back home. I imagine he regarded me as a novice in the realm of adoption and rather than simply acknowledge my feelings, he was compelled to insist on the group as cure-all for my angst. I do believe that peer self-help groups are quite important especially early on as a birth mother begins breaking her denial and moving toward self-acceptance. I'd been to a few meetings in my town as I'd needed, and felt I'd gotten what I needed at the time. But the well meaning expert presumed to know what I required without knowing me at all. As the session closed, another participant took me by the arm to tell me how to begin my own support group if I couldn't find one. I wearily thanked her for her advice and left the room.

Adoption conferences are a wonderful resource in terms of support, of being with people who speak the same language, who share so much in common. I was surprised that even here, in the safest and most comfortable of places in which to be a birth mother, I felt difficulty in being heard. I later read an article by Jane Calbreath whose words resonated with my own experiences:

> "Part of what still haunts me as a birth mother is
> that I was told, and I believed, that I had no value
> to the daughter that I relinquished. I understood
> that I was of no consequence to my baby. I could
> be replaced and forgotten. I was inconsequential.
> That feeling still lived deep inside of me twenty
> years later. I feared it might be true.

I have experienced feeling insignificant and unnecessary in other areas of my life. I have only just realized it reminds me of being told I wasn't important in my daughter's life."[1]

Tangentially, I note a trend of late in which books by birth mothers are disparaged as weepy, narcissistic or unimaginative. These judgments are usually rendered by triad members or professionals in the adoption reform movement. It may be that we become so immersed in the issues closest to our hearts that the familiar themes become tiresome. Unfortunately, I am so attached to others' judgments of me that I am suddenly frozen for weeks on end, unable to write, as I see everything I've shared thus far in danger of being dismissed as just one more offering in the genre of weepy birth mother mewlings. And yet, why do I care so much about what others think of me? Choosing to feel intimidated just will not do. I realize that embarrassed silence, fear of disapproval or that what I say is inconsequential only serves to continue my sense of marginalization. I believe that first person accounts by birth mothers offer inspiration and solidarity to mothers who have not yet "come out."

As Wayne Muller writes in *Legacy of the Heart*, "..many of us develop a deep ambivalence about being seen or known by others. Using our invisibility as a shield against pain, we become comfortable in our anonymity and unsure about how close or intimate we really want to be, even with those closest to us. Even as we feel handicapped by our separateness, at the same time we ache to be made whole with our friends, our family, and with God. We experience a deep, profound knowing that we do not belong in exile. We sense the possibility of a rich connection with others - yet we feel confused about where we belong, and mistrust that we will ever be welcome. For those of us who habitually withdraw in order to feel safe, our ability to feel part of a larger whole is clumsy and impaired. Reluctantly, and with great fear, we gradually make our home in isolation."[2]

Authenticity and openness connect us with our deepest selves as well as with others. Estes' words are instructive for a woman who grieves the relinquishment of her child:

> "The way to change a tragic drama back into a heroic one is to open the secret, speak of it to someone, write another ending, examine one's part in it and one's attributes in enduring it. These learnings are equal parts pain and wisdom. The having lived through it is a triumph of the deep and wild spirit.
>
> The shame-based secrets women carry are old, old tales. Any person who has kept a secret to her own detriment has been buried by shame. In this universal plight, the pattern itself is archetypal: the heroine has either been forced to do something or, through the loss of instinct, has been trapped into something. Typically, she is powerless to aright the sad condition. She is in some way sworn or shamed into secrecy. She complies for fear of loss of love, loss of regard, loss of basis subsistence. To seal the secret further, a curse is placed upon the person or persons who would reveal it. A terrible something or other is threatened if the secrecy is revealed.
>
> Women have been advised that certain events, choices, and circumstances in their lives, usually having to do with sex, love, money, violence and/or other difficulties rampant in the human condition, are of the most shameful nature and therefore completely without absolution. This is untrue."[3]

Letting go of our attachment to others' approval helps build our faith and courage. The language of adoption is replete with loaded terms that make implicit judgments. One term that comes to mind is "passive search" which refers to activities such as signing up with reunion registries that match searching parties. For a long time I felt slightly inadequate for not having mounted a more "active" search. My own process of enlisting with registries to make it easier should my daughter try to find me; writing to the adoption agency to provide an update on my whereabouts and requesting a social study of the adoptive parents; writing the hospital where she had been born for my records were significant, meaningful and therapeutic steps for me. I searched exactly as I needed to, at the pace I could handle. I went to several support group meetings when I felt I needed such contact and that suited my needs. What was right for me might be insufficient for another. That's OK. I do not believe that one or another method or pace is right or wrong. Individuals have different temperaments, needs, personal styles, personal histories and a variety of strengths and vulnerabilities. We grow as fast, act as fast, develop insights as fast as we can. Growth simply cannot be foisted onto people. Wisdom resides in every human soul. It tends to surface when given acceptance, encouragement, gentle direction and respect.

LATE DISCOVERY ADOPTEES

Over lunch today, my companion confides that one of her husband's relatives has never been told she was adopted. My friend was shocked when she learned from her husband that this woman in her early thirties, expecting her first child, is completely ignorant about her adoption although the rest of the family are aware that she was adopted as an infant. My friend hates being part of the family edict to keep the secret. We ponder her plight as a co-conspirator, the implicit mind-boggling betrayal and arrogant disrespect toward the unaware adoptee. I tell her that among the various support groups in the adoption constellation there is a subset of "late discovery adoptees" who found out later in life, usually by happenstance, that they were adopted. I suppose this is an effort to reassure her, or myself, that there is support for people like her husband's relative should this information surface, which seems to me is only a matter of time. Secret stuff has a way of oozing out. Sometimes secrets explode. Secret keepers in the world of adoption play a dangerous, and heartless, game.

MYTH

So entrenched is the myth of adoption as a uniformly and uncategorically joyous event, that I am frustrated when my efforts to communicate some of the complexities and pain of adoption are misunderstood or unheard. At such times images of the ghost self surface in my mind. My faltering attempts to explain my point of view appear to be received by listeners as meaningless, unclear, confused, or evidence of my personal neurosis. Unhappily, I find this reaction is as common among mental health professionals as any other group.

I am at a social event with women my age, among them social workers and counselors. I am describing my doctoral research on the long-term effects of relinquishing an infant for adoption. I say that the chronic grief and diminished self-esteem of many of the 54 women in my study mirrors my own experience of birth and surrender of my first baby. I think I am reasonably composed although such discussions generally cause my heart to race a bit. Plodding along anyway, I point out that my research covers only one aspect of adoption which is a vast topic. I say that I chose to look at the effects of relinquishment on birth mothers in closed adoptions because that was my own personal experience, although most triad members struggle to one degree or another with grief, loss, identity. Later in the evening as we say our goodbyes, the hostess, herself a psychotherapist, tells me excitedly about friends of hers, a couple in their fifties, who will soon travel to another country to adopt a baby. Inwardly I wince while murmuring some socially correct response. But I am seething. Did she not hear anything I said? I suppose it isn't realistic to think that friends of the adoptive couple are going to give much thought to the birth mother or the circumstances that will lead her to give her baby to strangers. Who am I to argue with the rescue of infants from orphanages? It would be rude, and not even entirely what I believe anyway, to point out that international adoption is perceived by some as cultural genocide. There are many reasons people choose to adopt internationally, sometimes out of a spiritual or "one world, one people" outlook.[1] But in my view, humanitarian action would involve helping improve conditions in those countries in which poverty or other dislocation results in separation of babies from families rather than exporting the babies for adoption. Janice Raymond has written a horrifying expose of reproductive technologies and the exploitation of women, including the abuses in international adoption. As she says "...many persons wanting to adopt sincerely desire to be good parents, but personal goodwill is not the only issue here. We must place the discussion of intercountry adoption in a social and political context and acknowledge that much more is at stake than a personal goal to parent. To argue for the welfare of a particular child should not justify practices that will, in the long run, place many children, women and cultures at risk.[2]

Those unacquainted with the world of adoption may not wonder about the challenges that will be experienced by the baby or small child transported to another culture. Unless one is personally interested in the topic of adoption, there is little awareness that international adoption has had some terrible problems. Babb, a respected adoption professional, states: "Adoption facilitators eager for financial gain have used coercive and illegal means of obtaining adoptable infants for American couples. Some facilitators in foreign countries such as Guatamala have gone so far as to have non-related women pose as surrendering birth mothers of stolen infants. Reputable agencies have had to resort to DNA testing and other means of proving that infants have been relinquished for adoption legally."[3] In a discussion of the conflicting views on international adoption, Freundlich notes that "There appears to be a strong relationship between the limited social and economic power of women in developing countries and the practices of international adoption. It is clear that poverty and low social status typify the backgrounds of the women who place their children for adoption internationally."[4] She also comments that "Although some characterize the women who place their children for adoption as simply lacking the capacity to rear their children...such incapacity in reality appears to be more closely associated with economic and social distress than with parenting ability or interest."[5]

In October 2000 the Hague Convention on Intercountry Adoptions was signed into law with the United States enacting the Intercountry Adoption Act of 2000. Safeguards are being put into place against child trafficking and fraud. Other abuses in international adoption that are addressed in this legislation include the non-disclosure or falsification of medical information, baby smuggling and obtaining consents under coercion.[6]

Sometimes I think about the complexities of adoption and how intensely personal the issues become once you are touched by it. I think about prospective adoptive parents who do weigh the possible negative effects and pitfalls of removing a child from his or her birth culture. I realize there are adoptive parents who honor and respect the child's birth culture and birth relations, conveying this attitude to their children. My frustration is a response to the unequivocally rosy picture painted by those who do not give much thought or even credence to the suffering of the child or the original mother. We hold onto the romantic notion of rescuing needy children in other parts of the world and how grateful those kids should be. Do you have to be an adoptee to relate to the terror of abandonment or dislocation that may be felt by the child? Do you have to be a birth mother to wonder about the desperation of women in other countries who lose their children this way?

A while back our local paper featured a woman who has arranged the adoptions of Russian children. The reader was left to conclude that there is no downside to this phenomenon. A reference to the children's grief was quickly followed by assurances that all 65 Russian "orphans" (some of whom had single parents who voluntarily put their children in the orphanage) had been successfully adopted.[7]

I find myself wondering about the huge number of children in the United States already freed for adoption who linger in foster care. How is it that couples will go to Russia, China, South America and other countries when children in the United States wait for permanent homes? I envision the small, serious faces of children I've counseled who were referred to therapy by foster care agencies. They are beautiful but troubled spirits, considered "too old" to be adoptable, or with too many special needs because of experiences in the disordered families of their birth. These are the euphemistically dubbed "waiting children" who ask why, if they can't go back to mom or dad or with relatives, can't there be another family who would want them? Adoption makes more sense to me when it is about children like these, who will not ever go back to their birth parents and who need permanent families.

My ideas continue to evolve over time as I amend, contradict, or affirm earlier opinions, and as I listen to the disparate voices of birth mothers, adoptees, adoptive parents. My quest is to develop emotionally, mentally and spiritually to the point where I can accept points of view about adoption which I find distasteful without becoming quite so incensed. I am still hoping to acquire a more nonchalant attitude but in the meantime I react, my gut response overwhelming intellect.

This comment is from a book for couples considering international adoption:

> "Another reason why we went international is
> that we were uncomfortable about the birthparent

issue. We had concerns with domestic adoption in that respect, not knowing what a relationship with a birthparent might be. With intercountry adoption, we knew that issue would probably not be there for us."[8]

No, the "issue" would be disappeared, as if she hadn't ever given birth at all.

In a chatty first person account of her experience with open, interracial adoption, an adoptive mother daydreams about the letter she really would have wanted to write to the birth mother in the process of finding a child. "Who are you, anyhow? What kind of person would get herself knocked up by a scummy guy who runs away when he hears the news? Haven't you heard of birth control? Of AIDS? Of abortion? Of OB GYNs? Of monogamy? Of love? I don't want my kid to be your mistake."[9]

The author assures the reader that this merely a fantasy and she has received kudos from reviewers for her honesty. For a moment I consider the revenge that could be extracted by writing an irreverent but brutally honest letter from a birth mother to the adoptive parents. As it happens, a parody of this sort just doesn't feel at all satisfying. I am mostly left wondering how the birth mother of her son would feel if she should read this book with the adoptive mother's secret thoughts about mothers like her.

There are a chorus of voices from adoption industry apologists and lobbyists who deny the pain inherent in adoption. An attorney and mother of children adopted internationally scoffs at the sorrow of all triad members - adoptees, birth mothers and infertile couples. She claims "Birth parents are conditioned to think that they *SHOULD* feel lifelong pain as the result of their 'unnatural' act of giving up their 'own' child for another to raise."[10] This is an astonishing statement, given that women my age who relinquished were told exactly the opposite: to forget the past and move on. Any conditioning had to do with the encouragement of denial and repression as defenses. Her statement also begs the question of who really believes that giving away one's infant is not an unnatural act? I will concede that under certain tragic circumstances it may be necessary, but does that make it natural?

The same writer thinks that "the infertile are conditioned to think that they *SHOULD* forever grieve over their inability to reproduce biologically."[11] But what of the genuine desperation and sadness of women who have longed to conceive and have been unable to do so? This is not an insignificant point because lack of resolution over infertility is a key to the shattered expectations seen so often in troubled adoptions where the adoptee can never be the longed for fantasy child.

I would not assume that lifelong agony over infertility is a given, especially for those who seek help through education and the resources that are currently available. No one in the adoption triad should feel they are consigned to a lifetime of pain. This does not mean, however, that there may not be issues that surface at different points over a lifetime as reminders of loss are presented.

An article on infertility by Patricia Johnston points out the importance of doing "the difficult but necessary work of dealing with loss proactively. When we don't do this work, we become victims or drifters in infertility, and it is victims or drifters who can be knocked off their feet by the emotional aftershocks of infertility."[12]

It is a common fiction that there are no problems with adoption per se but only problems when a child is placed in an unhealthy adoptive home environment. Adopted children do have distinct emotional and psychological hurdles. To acknowledge that there are specific developmental issues that apply to adoptees does not pathologize the adoptee. To deny or ignore the differences of being adopted dishonors the adoptee's reality and makes it so much more difficult for the child, adolescent or struggling adopted adult to seek help when it is appropriate.

The mind-set that minimizes problems of triad members is common among adoptive parents and people who arrange adoptions. I maintain that adoption begins with tragedy and this is true whether or not the birth mother professes to be pleased with the outcome. Relinquishing mothers in this day and age may have more of a voice in the process and sometimes choose the family for their child. When true openness is achieved between adoptive and birth families this is certainly beneficial for the adoptee. This does not alter the pathos embedded in the original broken bond.

❋

ADOPTION TODAY
(RELINQUISHMENT ADVICE)

There appears to be an adoption craze amongst celebrities. At the grocery checkout stand my eyes are drawn to headlines reporting the most recent actress to adopt an infant, or series of infants. Yesterday at the hair styling salon I pick up a popular magazine which lauds a well known model for hiring a surrogate to carry the baby she and her husband will raise (readers are happy to learn that the egg and sperm are from the couple so the baby is truly their progeny.) I wonder how much money the surrogate mother earned, and ruminate on how it happens that this practice is legal at all. Raymond has written about the myth of "the 'happy surrogate', a mainstay of the surrogate industry's advertising" which "has also become a regular feature of many newspaper articles."[1] Such articles are designed to counter the bad publicity arising out of court cases in which surrogates found it was not possible to conceive and bear a child and then give the child up. Quite apart from the ethical question of paying a woman to provide a baby, the more telling point is made by Nancy Verrier, author of *The Primal Wound*. Verrier's thesis on understanding the adopted child is based on research in pre and perinatal psychology, bonding and attachment theory. She explores the importance of prenatal bonding and the trauma that may be experienced by the infant suddenly separated from the familiar rhythms, smells, voices, and other sounds the infant has known in the mother's womb. Verrier asserts that "the wrong mother is labeled the surrogate in this practice. A woman who gives birth is the mother of that baby, not a surrogate mother...This distinction is very important, because it may be this complete reversal of truth which has given an air of legitimacy to the surrogacy program. If we call the real mother the surrogate mother, it makes it easier to deny her importance in her child's life..infants separated from their mothers suffer a narcissistic wound. Therefore it would seem obvious that to conceive a child with the *INTENTION* of separating from that child would be setting the child up for psychological distress. These mothers are not deliberately setting out to harm their children, they are just unaware of what the consequences will be when that connection is severed."[2]

Over my first cup of coffee this morning I read the usual glowing account of an actress in Hollywood who, with her husband, has adopted an infant born to an unwed mother in a southern state. Reminded again that rich people can buy whatever they want, and that poverty is the number one cause of relinquishment in modern times.[3] Current trends in infant adoption, both domestic and international, including assisted reproductive techniques and surrogacy, continue the move in adoption away from focus on the needs of the child for a permanent family to a business, money and power focus that serves the needs of adults (including a sense of entitlement about producing or finding a child).

In the old system of infant adoption, young unmarried mothers were coerced into relinquishment out of the shame and impropriety of an out of wedlock pregnancy. Today relinquishment rates are less than 3%. The social service agencies that used to place infants are nowadays primarily responsible for finding permanent homes for older, special needs children who have been freed for adoption. Most infant adoptions in the United States are now conducted by "adoption facilitators" and private attorneys. Adoption is a very lucrative business. Poor women are vulnerable to being pressured about the adoption of their infants because as so-called "adoptable" infants (healthy and white) are scarce, the trend is to recruit in the Bible Belt and other areas with high rates of poverty. Sometimes families with two or more children are relinquishing babies due to their economic problems.

It seems to me that viewing adoption as a cure for poverty is only possible in a system that denies the humanity of birth parents. Katha Pollitt comments on the popularity of adoption among both political liberals and conservatives, in terms of addressing poverty and teenage pregnancy. She notes:

> "There are good reasons why only 3 percent of white girls and 1 percent of black girls - and an even tinier percentage of adult women - choose adoption. Maybe more would do so if adoption were more fluid and open - a kind of open-ended "guardianship" arrangement - but that would discourage adoptive parents. The glory days of white baby relinquishment in the 1950s and 1960s depended on coercion - the illegality of abortion, the sexual double standard and the stigma of unwed motherhood, enforced by family, neighbors, school, social workers, medicine, church, law. Those girls gave up their babies because they had no choice - that's why we are now hearing from so many sad and furious 50-year old birth mothers. Do we really want to create a new generation of them by applying the guilt and pressure tactics that a behavior change of such magnitude would require?"[4]

She suggests that adoption as public policy avoids hard questions about poverty and sex, noting that if poverty is the problem, why not enact policies that would help mothers and children? And if teenage pregnancy is the problem why not promote contraception, sex education and health care?

The stigma and shame of the past have diminished but the single mother still faces the possibility of exploitation. Fraudulent crisis lines may act as fronts for attorneys who broker adoptions. In the marketplace for infants, merchandising techniques draw in unmarried pregnant girls and women. Looking in our local yellow pages under "Adoption" I see pictures of smiling adoption facilitators promising birth mothers that "all the choices are yours". One adoption facilitation center promotes college scholarships for birth mothers, among other free services. The coercive nature of these services is a reminder that the system is driven by adoptive parents, the paying consumers to whom agencies and attorneys cater. I notice, too, that the several of the attorneys also offer surrogacy services. Freundlich comments on the various marketing practices used in adoption and notes that "it provides an unsettling picture of the realities of contemporary adoption practice and raises questions regarding the extent to which market forces will shape adoption in the future."[5]

Pannor worries that "Open adoption, which is now the prevailing practice throughout the country has opened new doors that can help to move adoption in new and healthier directions. Unfortunately it is being used as a tool to seduce birthparents into giving up their children to adoption."[6]

Unmarried mothers need objective help in making a decision about relinquishment. Even when all of the ramifications and options are explored, relinquishment entails a profound loss. It is imperative that these clients be helped to examine all of their options and the possible long-term consequences of each: abortion, marriage, agency adoption, independent adoption, adoption by another family member or single parenthood. Ideally, the birth father and the birth parents' families of origin would be included in planning. Reitz and Watson point out that the mother should thoroughly explore the possibility of keeping her child or arranging for the child's care within the extended family. They point out:

> "This is not to denigrate the value of adoption,
> but rather to recognize its inherent limitations.
> As clinicians and agencies have come to

understand more clearly the importance of genetic ties and of the birth bond, as they have seen the difficulty grieving a child lost in adoption, and as they have come to realize through experience that adoption is not a magical solution for rearing children, they have begun to place greater emphasis on programs designed to preserve birth families."[7]

Today's unmarried mothers do have more choices yet the pressures are tremendous and the decision to place a child is terribly difficult. As Pavao says, it requires "abstract thinking about what giving up this child actually will be like, not just now, but forever. The decision to parent - often parent alone - requires equally abstract thinking...And either decision will last a lifetime and affect many lives."[8]

Reitz and Watson point out that the unmarried mother in crisis may want to deny the pain of her experience; in her ambivalence she may seize on only one option. A treatment plan with concrete action could include attention to prenatal care, gathering information from agencies to figure out what financial resources might be available and seeking out possible resources for housing, child care, and employment assistance if she herself raises her child. A teenager might visit a high school with a program for parenting teens. If adoption is a serious alternative she could be helped to make the most informed decision possible by locating birth parents, perhaps through a birth parent support group. Adoption related books with information specific to birth parent concerns would be helpful in the decision making process.

If the mother believes relinquishment is the best alternative she will need ethical help. What is the adoption agency or facilitator's philosophy about adoption? What can she expect after the baby is born? What if she decides she wants to parent after giving birth? If an attorney is used he or she should only represent the birth mother.

Babb reports that "The research on ethics in adoption shows that adoption, more than any other human service, is rife with conflict of interest. Adoption agency social workers and attorneys routinely represent both birth and adoptive families party to the same adoption. Agencies whose very existence is based on fees paid for consumated adoptions claim to offer unbiased 'crisis pregnancy' counseling to expectant mothers."[9]

The mother should find out if the attorney will be paid by the prospective adoptive parents if she decides she herself wants to keep the baby. She will need help with legal issues, such as ensuring that her baby is not placed in a home without an approved home study. She should get copies of all papers she signs; everything the agency or facilitator promises should be in writing.

The mother considering open adoption needs to be aware that there are degrees of openness ranging from some exchange of identifying information to more of an extended family arrangement with the adoptive parents having full legal parenting rights and the birth parent being a supportive presence in the child's life. An adoption agreement can establish the roles, responsibilities and boundaries for all parties. The birth mother needs to know that the agreements are not enforceable in most states and there is a degree of risk in that an 'open' adoption may become 'closed' once the adoption is finalized if the adoptive parents so choose.

One of the best books on open adoption, in terms of its practical help to those involved in it, and because of its deep compassion and emphasis on what is good for the child is *The Spirit of Open Adoption* by James Gritter. Gritter does not see open adoption as a panacea:

"Open adoption should not be oversold. It can work beautifully, but it does not erase the original pain. If people get the idea that open adoption relieves all the pain, they are certain to be disappointed. Open adoption is thoroughly painful and imperfect. It does not provide happy endings for every predicament. In many instances, there may be better alternatives. It is fair to say, however, that at least some of the time for some for some of the people, open adoption offers a warm and positive alternative."[10]

Babb cautions that "Professionals who arrange open adoptions should provide birth parents with complete and accurate information, including the legal enforceability or unenforceability of such adoptions. When exploring open adoption with birth parents, professionals should be careful that the promise of open adoption does not become a coercive means of encouraging the surrender of a child. Professionals should recognize the manipulative potential of open adoption during pregnancy and childbirth, and should consider the harmful effects of having prospective adoptive parents participate in an expectant mother's prenatal care, or be present at an infant's birth or at the hospital afterward. Birth parents should have the opportunity to experience parenthood without the onus of anxiety or guilt about the feelings of the prospective adoptive parents. The potential heartache of prospective adoptive parents with whom they have developed a predelivery relationship should not be used as a coercive means of obtaining the relinquishment of an infant."[11]

The business of adoption is in critical need of regulation. There is a risk of exploitation not only to the birth parents, but also to the prospective adopters. Pavao notes that "In grey market adoptions both sets of parents may be deceived and misguided, but the actual adoption is done legally, although brokers attempt to get around the law and to place babies with the highest bidder.

Independent adoptions can be either grey market or totally ethical and legal depending on the professionals doing them."[12] Concerning the growing alarm about current adoption policy and practices, Freundlich concludes "Powerful market forces are in play, but at the same time, professionals from all fields of adoption - infant adoption in the U.S., international adoption, and the adoption of children from the foster care system in this country - are raising questions about the ethics of current practice and challenging policies that may, in the past, have simply been tolerated. The environment indeed may be ripe for reshaping the forces that drive adoption."[13]

It is repugnant and unacceptable that the lack of adoption regulations in the United States too often results in babies being essentially sold to the highest bidder. It is unseemly at best, and dangerous at worst, to find babies by advertising in newspapers, magazines and the Internet. In many ways the current "system" is arguably even worse than the tragically flawed old system of relinquishment as rehabilitation. It serves neither the infant, the birth mother or society when external pressures such as poverty, lack of resources, lack of information or sheer exploitation influence the course of an unexpected pregnancy.

❀

EPILOGUE

"**I** think you've lived a soft life" my young client stated. Noting my questioning gaze she quickly went on, "Well, it's not a bad thing, I don't mean it that way, it's just that some people live hard, and some don't - like maybe they'd be happy being an accountant, or something." Surprise, irritation, amusement, tumble over each other in my mind as I contemplate a response. My reply is, I hope, a neutral invitation for her to continue. As she does, I half listen while I examine my own reaction. Countertransference is the personal, sometimes overly reactive inner response to a client, in this case her inference about me and my imagined soft life. I ask myself why her statement makes me feel defensive, hurt, annoyed. The truth is, now in my middle years I do have a relatively soft life, one filled with love and many other blessings, none of which I take for granted. In general, I am calmer now; reunion with my daughter has instilled in my heart greater peacefulness and immense gratitude. I found my laugh again. I have to acknowledge that my life is, in a good many respects, a privileged one. Yet, what I feel like sharing is "If you knew more about me you'd realize that like you, I've known hard times, and alienation, and a melancholy that never quite goes completely away." Having mentally processed this reaction my full attention returns to the expressive young woman across from me. I wonder what she, an adoptee, would think if she knew I was a birth mother: a woman still trying to reconcile the many paradoxes of mind and heart.

❃

CONTENT NOTES

NOTE TO READERS:

1. **Waldron, J.**, *Giving Away Simone*, New York Times Books, 1995, pg. xvi. I recommend this powerful and eloquent memoir. Waldron was 17 when she gave birth to Simone, whom she subsequently relinquished for adoption. Waldron says "The upside of the current confessional climate in this country, in which women who sin and tell populate television talk shows, is the undoing of a conspiracy to erase ourselves and the effort to give life to the stories we've been expected to hide. (There are millions of birthmothers in this country, yet most people will tell you they've never met ONE. Nearly as many will tell you they don't know what a birthmother is.") pg. xvii.

2. **Stiffler, L.**, *Synchronicity and Reunion*, FEA Publishing, Hobe Sound, Florida, 1992, pg. 172. Stiffler's doctoral research is the basis of this fascinating book. Reunited families describe meaningful, and often amazing, coincidences in correspondence of space, time and circumstance during their years of separation.

3. **Reyman, L.**, *Birth Mother Loss: Long-term Effects of Surrendering an Infant for Adoption with Implications for Treatment*, Ph.D. dissertation, California Coast University, Santa Ana, California 1999. Analysis of relinquishment factors and long-term effects showed significance in two areas. There was a significant relationship between the mother's sense of not having had a genuine choice and a decrease in self esteem. There was also a significant relationship between chronic grief and the belief that the relinquishment decision was not fully one's choice.

GHOST MOTHER:

1. **Doka, K. J.**, ed., *Disenfranchised Grief*, Lexington Books, New York, 1989. Contributors explore the hidden sorrows embedded in a myriad of losses, the nature of which deprive the grieving person of catharsis and comfort.

2. **Lifton, B.J.**, *Journey of the Adopted Self*, Basic Books, New York, 1994, pg. 11.

SEPARATION OF MOTHERS AND BABIES AS SOCIAL POLICY:

1. Most research in the field of adoption focuses on issues pertaining to adopted children and adoptive parents. The following are a sampling of studies that consider the long-term impact on mothers who relinquished in closed adoptions, where no identifying information is exchanged.

    Sorosky, A., Baran, A., Pannor, R., *The Adoption Triangle*, Anchor Press/Doubleday, New York, 1978. Until these researchers investigated the impact of sealed records on all members of the adoption triad there had been no follow-up studies on birth parents. Their research, presented to the American Psychological Association in 1976 was the basis for *The Adoption Triangle*. This group of 36 mothers and 2 fathers described chronic grief involving "...loss, pain and a continuing sense of caring for that long vanished child. In some cases a reunion would be accepted, in others it would be discouraged or refused. In all situations the intensity of feeling and involvement is clearly there." pg. 72.

    Burnell, G., and Norfleet, M., *"Women Who Place Their Infants for Adoption: A Pilot Study"* Patient Counseling Education, *1*, 169-172, 1979. A mail questionnaire was used to follow up on 300 women, members of the Kaiser-Permanente Plan, who in the previous three years had placed a child for adoption. A 26% response rate showed that gynecological, medical and psychiatric problems were present in about 60% of the subjects. The most common emotional disorder identified was depression (40% of the respondents.)

Rynearson, E., *"Relinquishment and Its Maternal Complications: A Preliminary Study"*, American Journal of Psychiatry, Vol. 139, 1982, pg. 338-340. A group of 20 outpatients were interviewed regarding the effects of relinquishment. These white, middle class women ranging in age from 30 to 46 had surrendered their first child between 15 and 19 years of age while they were unmarried. Rynearson found that the mother's loss is "irresolvable because the child continues to exist," pg. 338. The subjects believed their decision to be "externally enforced" and belied their wish to keep their babies. Nineteen of his subjects entertained rescue fantasies in which the mother and baby would be "saved" from relinquishment. Defenses of denial, repression and fantasy were common. All of the subjects reported numbing and dissociation during hospitalization. Signing the adoption papers was traumatic and symbolized the act of surrender. Post-relinquishment effects included fear of future infertility, varying degrees of sexual dysfunction, and anniversary reactions such as intensified mourning, particularly on occasions such as the child's birthdate.

Deykin, E., Campbell, L., and Patti, P., *"The Postadoption Experience of Surrendering Parents"*, American Journal of Orthopsychiatry, Vol. 54, no. 2, 1984, pg. 271-280. 321 birth mothers and 13 birth fathers answered a survey questionnaire. Results of the study revealed that respondents continued to grieve over time. The relinquishment experience, for the majority of this group, had significant effects on subsequent life functioning. External factors such as family opposition to keeping the baby and pressure from social workers to relinquish were cited by 69% of the sample as the primary reasons for surrender of the child.

Fonda, A. B., *"Birth Mothers Who Search: An Exploratory Study"*, Dissertation Abstracts International, 4502B, University Microfilms No. 84-11248, 1984. A descriptive study of 12 birth mothers revealed the impact of relinquishment and the need to search for the lost child. Pressures to conceal their pregnancies and the expectation that they would resume life in the community post-relinquishment with no acknowledgment of loss appeared linked to the need to search. Fonda concludes that relinquishment exerts a profound impact on the mother's self concept and that searching may be a way to resolve the trauma of relinquishment.

Condon, J. T., *"Psychological Disability in Women Who Relinquish a Baby For Adoption"*, The Medical Journal of Australia, vol. 144, February 3, 1986, pg. 117-119. A group of twenty mothers were studied with a mean time of 21 years since relinquishment. In comparison with an age-matched control group, the relinquishing mothers rated significantly higher on depression and psychosomatic symptoms. A key finding was that the majority of women reported no decrease in feelings of anger, sadness and guilt since relinquishment.

McAdoo, L. L., *"Birthmothers: The Forgotten Link of the Adoption Triangle"*, Ph.D. dissertation, University of New Mexico, 1992. The subjects were 41 women who had relinquished children between 1929 and 1990. Sixty one percent of women reported that they had placed their child because they had no other choice. The women who reported the strongest sense of autonomy in the decision were significantly more likely to believe the decision was good one.

Edwards, D. S., *"Transformations of Motherhood in Adoption: The Experiences of Relinquishing Mothers"*, Ph.D. dissertation, University of Florida, 1995. Forty-six women who had relinquished 16 to 51 years prior were interviewed. Themes uncovered were rejection by the birthfather and pressure from social work professionals as strong factors in the decision to place the child. Relinquishment was reported as the most traumatic event of the subjects' lives.

Weintraub, M. and Kostan, V., *"Birthmothers: Silent*

Relationships", *Journal of Women and Social Work*, 1995, Fall, vol. 10, no. 3. Interviews with eight relinquishing mothers reported emotional pain, isolation and secrecy; self-blame and stigmatization; relationship failures and depression; temporary inhibition of development; disappointment with mental health practitioners.

DeSimone, M., *"Birthmother Loss: Contributing Factors to Unresolved Grief"*, *Clinical Social Work Journal*, vol. 24, no. 1, Spring, 1996, pg. 65-76. 264 women were studied who had placed infants for adoption. The majority of participants were 19 years or younger at the time of surrender. Predictors of high levels of unresolved grief included the belief that their relinquishment decision was not completely their own; high levels of guilt and shame over the relinquishment; and an inadequate opportunity to express their feelings about the relinquishment.

2. **Millen, L. and Roll, S.**, *"Solomon's Mothers: A Special Case of Pathological Bereavement"*, *American Journal of Orthopsychiatry*, vol. 55, no. 3, 1985, pg. 413. The authors' illustrate how the bereavement process was distorted and delayed in 22 women seen in psychotherapy who had earlier relinquished a child.

3. Ibid., pg. 414.

4. **Vought, J.**, *Post-Abortion Trauma*, Zondervan Publishing House, Grand Rapids, Michigan, 1991.

5. **Slife, B.**, ed., *Taking Sides: Clashing Views on Controversial Psychological Issues*, tenth edition, Dushkin/McGraw Hill, Guilford, Connecticut, 1998, pg. 328-350. A good summary of opposing arguments regarding post abortion effects is presented.

6. **Solinger, R.**, *Wake Up Little Susie: Single Pregnancy and Race Before Roe v. Wade*, Routledge, New York, 1992. This is a fascinating and meticulously researched book which

includes the first published analysis of maternity homes in the United States 1945-1965.

7.   **Solinger, R.**, Ibid., pg. 7.

8.   **Coontz, S.**, *The Way We Never Were*, Harper Collins, New York, 1992. Coontz provides historical evidence that counters illusions about our past. For example, the family-oriented 1950s were the peak years in United State history for teenage childbearing.

9.   **Wegar, K.**, *Adoption, Identity and Kinship*, Yale University, New Haven, Connecticut, 1997.

10.   **McGoldrick M., Giordano, J., Pearce, J. K.**, *Ethnicity and Family Therapy*, Guilford Press, New York, 1996.

11.   **Harvey, B.**, *The Fifties: A Women's Oral History*, Harper Collins, New York, 1993.

12.   **Coontz, S.**, *The Way We Never Were*, pg. 237.

13.   **Coontz, S.**, Ibid., pg. 238.

14.   **Coontz, S.**, Ibid., pg. 239.

15.   **Wegar, K.**, *Adoption, Identity and Kinship*, pg. 24.

16.   **McGoldrick, M., M. Giordano, J., Pearce, J. K.**, *Ethnicity and Family Therapy*, pg. 59-60.

17.   **Solinger, R.**, *Wake Up Little Susie: Single Pregnancy and Race Before Roe v. Wade*, pg. 27.

18.   **Schertz, F.**, *"Taking Sides in the Unmarried Mother's Conflict"*, in *Journal of Social Casework*, 1947, vol. 28, pg. 47.

19.   **Schertz, F.**, Ibid., pg. 100.

20. **Solinger, R.**, *Abortion Wars - A Half Century of Struggle 1950-2000*, University of California Press, Berkeley, California, 1998.

21. **Young, L.**, *Out of Wedlock*, McGraw Hill, New York, 1954.

22. **Mantecon, V.**, *"The Effects of Relinquishment and Reunion on a Family System"*. Presented at the American Association for Marriage and Family Therapy, Anaheim, California, October, 1993.

23. **Chesler, P.**, *Sacred Bond*, Times Books, New York, 1988, pg. 120.

A WINDOW OF TIME:

1. **Franklin, L.**, *May the Circle Be Unbroken*, Random House, New York, 1998, pg. 17. Franklin provides a comprehensive look at adoption from the perspective of all triad members.

2. **Taylor, P.**, *Shadow Train*, Gateway Press, Baltimore, Maryland, 1995, pg. xiii. Taylor, a therapist as well as a birth mother, looks at the impact of her relinquishment experience from a family systems point of view.

3. **O'Reilly, J.**, *"Mother and Child Reunion"* in Mirabella, Oct. 1991, pg. 148.

4. **Estes, C. P.**, *Women Who Run With the Wolves: Myths and Stories of the Wild Woman Archetype*, Ballantine Books, New York, 1992, pg. 173. Estes' treasure of a book is relevant to all women, and perhaps is especially meaningful to adoptees and birth mothers.

DOING TIME:

1. **Solinger, R.**, *Wake Up Little Susie: Single Pregnancy and Race Before Roe v. Wade*, Rutledge, New York, 1992, pg. 134.

TRIGGERS:

1. **Teller, D.**, *"Shame On Us: How Shame Affects the Sexuality and Intimacy of Birthmothers"* Presented at American Adoption Southwest Regional Conference, San Francisco, Nov. 14, 1998.

2. See for example: **Jones, M. B.**, *Birth Mothers: Women Who Relinquished Babies for Adoption Tell Their Stories*, Review Press, Chicago, 1993; **Taylor, P.**, *Shadow Train*, Gateway Press, Baltimore, Maryland, 1995; **Carlini, H.**, *Birth Mother Trauma*, Morning Side Publishing, Toronto, 1992; **Soll, J.**, *Adoption Healing*, Gateway Press, Baltimore, Maryland, 2000; **Russell, M.**, *Adoption Wisdom*, Broken Branch Productions, Santa Monica, California, 1996; **Riben**, *The Dark Side of Adoption*, Harlo Press, Detroit, 1988.

3. *Diagnostic and Statistical Manual IV*, Fourth Edition, American Psychiatric Association, 1994, Washington, D.C., pgs. 424-429.

4. **Jones, M. B.**, *Birth Mothers: Women Who Relinquished Babies for Adoption Tell Their Stories*, Review Press, Chicago, Illinois, 1993, pgs. 272-273.

BIRTH MOTHER AS WIMP:

1. **Gritter, J.**, *The Spirit of Open Adoption*, Child Welfare League of America Press, Washington, D.C., 1997.

CUTOFFS:

1. "If a birthmother feels shame, it is probably from some early belief about herself, not because of the relinquishment. Relinquishment is an act, which might lead to guilt." **Verrier, N.**, *The Primal Wound*, Gateway Press, Baltimore, Maryland, 1993, pg. 191.

THERAPY:

1. **Solinger, R.**, *Abortion Wars, A Half Century of Struggle 1950-2000*, University of California Press, Berkeley,

California, 1998, pg. 28.

2.   **Coontz, S.**, *The Way We Never Were*, Harper Collins, New York, 1992.

3.   **Ludtke, M.**, *On Our Own, Unmarried Mothers in America*, Random House, New York, 1997.

4.   **Lawson, A. and Rhode, D.**, editors, *The Politics of Pregnancy, Adolescent Sexuality and Public Policy*, Yale University Press, New Haven and London, 1993.

5.   **Roles, P.**, *Saying Goodbye to a Baby: Vol. 1, The Birth Parents Guide to Loss and Grief in Adoption*, Child Welfare League, Washington, D.C., 1989, pg. 25. Roles, herself a birth mother and social worker, offers compassionate and sound advice for the unmarried pregnant mother in the first of two volumes. *Saying Goodbye to a Baby, Vol. 2* is a counselor's guide to birth parent loss and grief in adoption.

6.   **Brodzinsky, A.**, *"Surrendering an Infant for Adoption: The Birthmother Perspective"* in D.M. Brodzinsky and M. Schechter (editors) *Psychology of Adoption*, Oxford University Press, New York, 1990.

7.   **Millen, L. and Roll, S.**, Ibid., pg. 418.

8.   **Reyman, L.**, *"Birth Mother Loss: Long-Term Effects of Surrendering an Infant for Adoption with Implications for Treatment"*, pg. 64.

9.   **Reyman, L.**, Ibid.

10. **Herman, J.**, *Trauma and Recovery*, Basic Books, New York, 1992, pg. 3.

11. **Fonda, A. B.**, *"Birthmothers Who Search: An Exploratory Study"* Dissertation Abstracts International. 450B. University

Microfilms No. 84-11248.

12. **Gediman, J. S. and Brown, L. P.** Birth Bond, New Horizons, Far Hills, New Jersey, 1989. A fascinating study of reunited pairs. Helpful for identifying the issues that commonly surface as birth parent and adoptee navigate their relationship after reunion. A good resource.

13. **Carlini, H.**, *Birth Mother Trauma*, Morning Side Publishing, Toronto, 1992.

14. **Klein, C. and Gotti, R.**, *Overcoming Regret*, Bantam Books, New York, 1992.

15. **Stiffler, L.**, *Synchronicity and Reunion*, FEA Publishing, Hobe Sound, Florida, 1992, pg. 3.

16. **Muller, W.**, *Legacy of the Heart: The Spiritual Advantages of a Painful Childhood.* Simon and Schuster, New York, 1992, pg. xv. Muller offers a compassionate approach to the transformation of pain into wisdom, healing and love.

THE HEALING WORKSHOP:

1. **Calbreath, J.**, *"On Feeling Insignificant"* in *Pact Press*, San Francisco, California, Winter 1997, pg. 11.

2. **Muller, W.**, *Legacy of the Heart: The Spiritual Advantage of a Painful Childhood*, pg. 156.

3. **Estes, C. P.**, <u>*Women Who Run With the Wolves: Myths and Stories of the Wild Woman Archetype*</u>, Ballantine Books, New York, 1992, pgs. 376-377.

MYTH:

1. **Knoll, J. and Murphy, M. K.**, *International Adoption: Sensitive Advice for Prospective Parents*, Chicago Review Press, 1992, pg. 10.

2. **Raymond, J.**, *Women as Wombs: Reproductive Technologies and the Battle Over Women's Freedom*, 1993, Harper Collins, New York, pg. 152.

3. **Babb, L. A.**, *Ethics in American Adoption*, Bergin and Garvey, Westport, Connecticut, 1999, pg. 48.

4. **Freundlich, M.**, *"The Market Forces in Adoption"* in *Adoption and Ethics*, Child Welfare League of America, The Evan B. Donaldson Institute, Washington, D.C., pg. 53.

5. Ibid.

6. **Hoard C.**, *"U.S. Implements Hague Convention"* in *American Adoption Congress Decree*, Fall 2000, pg. 14.

7. *"Transplanting Love From Siberia"* in *Enterprise-Record/Mercury-Register*, Jan. 17, 2000, pg. 1B.

8. *International Adoption: Sensitive Advice for Prospective Parents*, Chicago Review Press, pg. 56.

9. **Wolff, J.**, *Secret Thoughts of an Adoptive Mother*, Andrews and McMeel, Kansas City, pg. 17.

10. **Bartholet, E.**, *Family Bonds*, Houghton Mifflin, Boston, Massachusetts, 1993, pg. 182.

11. Ibid.

12. **Johnston, P.**, *"Infertility and Aftershocks"* in *Pact Press*, San Francisco, 1997, pg. 5

ADOPTION TODAY (RELINQUISHMENT ADVICE):

1. **Raymond, J.**, *Women as Wombs: Reproductive Technologies and the Battle Over Women's Freedom*, Harper Collins, New York, 1993, pg. 113.

2. **Verrier, N.**, *The Primal Wound*, Gateway Press, Baltimore, Maryland, 1997, pg. 205.

3. **Pannor, R.**, *"Going Beyond...Open Records and Open Adoption"* from interview cited in *CUB Communicator*, Winter 2000/2001, pg. 3.

4. **Pollitt, K.**, *"Adoption Fantasy"* in *The Nation*, 72 Fifth Ave., N.Y., July 8, 1996.

5. **Freundlich, M.**, *"The Market Forces in Adoption"* in *Adoption and Ethics*, Vol. 2, Child Welfare League of America, The Evan B. Donaldson Adoption Institute, Washington, D.C., 2000, pg.120. This is one of a four volume series on adoption. An excellent resource for adoption professionals.

6. **Pannor, R.**, *"Going Beyond...Open Records and Open Adoption"*, pg. 3.

7. **Reitz, M. and Watson, K. W.**, editors, *Adoption and the Family System*, Guilford Press, New York, pg. 70.

8. **Pavao, J. M.**, *The Family of Adoption*, Beacon Press, Boston, Massachusetts, 1998, pg. 199.

9. **Babb, A. L.**, *Ethics in American Adoption*, pg. 1

10. **Gritter, J.**, *The Spirit of Open Adoption*, pg. 23.

11. **Babb, A. L.**, *Ethics In American Adoption*, pg. 148.

12. **Pavao, J. M.**, *The Family of Adoption*, Beacon Press, Boston, Massachusetts, 1998, pg. 96.

13. **Freundlich, M.**, *"The Market Forces in Adoption"* in *Adoption and Ethics*, Child Welfare League of America, The Evan B. Donaldson Inst., Washington, D.C., 2000, pg. 121.

BIBLIOGRAPHY

Babb, L. A., *Ethics in American Adoption*, Connecticut, Bergin & Garvey, Westport, Connecticut, 1999.

Bartholet, E., *Family Bonds*, Houghton Mifflin, Boston, 1993.

Brodzinsky, A. B., "Surrendering an Infant for Adoption: The Birthmother Perspective" in D.M. Brodzinsky & M. Schecter (eds.), *Psychology of Adoption*. New York: Oxford University Press, 1990.

Burnell, G. & Norfleet, M., *Women Who Place Their Infants for Adoption: A Pilot Study. Patient Education Counseling*, 1, 169-172, 1979.

Calbreath, J., *"On Feeling Insignificant"* in Pact Press, San Francisco, California, Winter, 997.

Carlini, H., *Birth Mother Trauma*, Morning Side Publishing, Toronto, 1992.

Chesler, P., *Sacred Bond*. Times Books, New York, 1988.

Condon, J. T., *"Psychological Disability in Women Who Relinquish a Baby for Adoption"*, *Medical Journal of Australia*, Vol. 144, February 3, 1986.

Coontz, S., *The Way We Never Were*, Harper Collins, New York, 1992.

DeSimone, M., "Birthmother Loss: Contributing Factors to Unresolved Grief", in *Clinical Social Work Journal*, 24(1), 1996.

Deykin, E., Campbell, L., & Patti, P., "The Postadoption Experience of Surrendering Parents" in *American Journal of Orthopsychiatry*, 54(2), 271-280, 1984.

Diagnostic and Statistical Manual IV, Fourth Edition, American Psychiatric Association, Washington, D.C., 1994.

Doka, K., *Disenfranchised Grief*, Lexington Books, New York, 1989.

Edwards, D.S., *Transformations of Motherhood in Adoption: The Experiences of Relinquishing Mothers*, Ph.D. dissertation, University of Florida, 1995.

Enterprise Record/Mercury-Register, "Transplanting Love From Siberia", Chico, California, January 17, 2000.

Estes, C. P., *Women Who Run With the Wolves: Myths and Stories of the Wild Woman Archetype*, Ballantine Books, New York, 1992.

Fonda, A. B., *Birthmothers Who Search: An Exploratory Study*. Dissertation Abstracts International, 4502B. (University Microfilms No. 84-11248), 1984.

Franklin, L., *May The Circle Be Unbroken*, Random House, New York, 1998.

Freundlich, M., "The Market Forces in Adoption" in *Adoption and Ethics*, Child Welfare League of America, The Even B. Donaldson Institute, Washington, D.C., 2000.

Gediman, J. S. & Brown, L. P., *Birth Bond*, New Horizons, Far Hills, New Jersey, 1989.

Gritter, J., *The Spirit of Open Adoption*, Child Welfare League of America Press, Washington, D.C., 1997.

Harvey, B., *The Fifties: A Woman's Oral History*, Harper Collins, New York, 1993.

Herman, J., *Trauma and Recovery*, Basic Books, New York, 1992.

Hoard, C., "U.S. Implements Hague Convention" in Decree, American Adoption Congress, Washington, D.C., 2000.

Johnston, P. I., "Infertility and Aftershocks" in Pact Press, San Francisco, California, 1997.

Jones, M. B., *Birth Mothers: Women Who Relinquished Babies for Adoption Tell Their Stories*, Review Press, Chicago, 1993.

Klein, C. & Gotti, R., *Overcoming Regret*, Bantam Books, New York, 1992.

Knoll, J. & Murphy, M. K., *"International Adoption: Sensitive Advice for Prospective Parents"*, Chicago Review Press, Chicago, Illinois, 1994.

Lawson, A. & Rhode, eds., *The Politics of Pregnancy, Adolescent Sexuality and Public Policy.* Yale University Press, New Haven, Connecticut, 1993.

Lifton, B. J., *Journey of the Adopted Self*, Basic Books, New York, 1994.

Ludtke, M., *On Our Own: Unmarried Mothers in America*, Random House, New York, 1997.

McAdoo, L. L., *Birthmothers: The Forgotten Link of the Adoption Triangle*, Ph.D. dissertation, University of New Mexico, 1992.

McGoldrick, M., Giordano, J., Pearce, J. K., *Ethnicity and Family Therapy*, Guilford Press, New York, 1996.

Mantecon, V., *The Effects of Relinquishment and Reunion on a Family System.* Presented at American Association for Marriage and Family Therapy, Anaheim, California, October 1993.

Millen, L. & Roll, S., "Solomon's Mothers: A Special Case of Pathological Bereavement", in *American Journal of Orthopsychiatry*, 55(3), 411-418, 1985.

Muller, W., *Legacy of the Heart: The Spiritual Advantages of a Painful Childhood*, Simon & Schuster, New York, 1992.

O'Reilley, J., "Mother and Child Reunion" in Mirabella, 1991.

Pannor, R., "Going Beyond...Open Records & Open Adoption" in CUB Communicator, Encinitas, California, Winter 2000/2001.

Pavao, J. M., *The Family of Adoption*, Beacon Press, Boston, Massachusetts, 1998.

Pollitt, K., "Adoption Fantasy" in The Nation, New York, 1996.

Raymond J., *Women as Wombs: Reproductive Technologies and the Battle Over Women's Freedom*, Harper Collins, New York, 1993.

Reitz, M. & Watson, K., *Adoption and the Family System*, Guilford Press, New York, 1992.

Reyman, L., *Birth Mother Loss: Long-term Effects of Surrendering an Infant for Adoption with Implications for Treatment*, Ph.D. dissertation, California Coast University, Santa Ana, California, 1999.

Riben, M., *The Dark Side of Adoption*, Harlo, Detroit, Michigan, 1988.

Roles, P., *Saying Goodbye to a Baby: Vol. 1, The Birth Parents Guide to Loss and Grief in Adoption*, Child Welfare League of America, Washington, D.C., 1989.

Rynearson, E., "Relinquishment and its Maternal Complications: A Preliminary Study", in *American Journal of Psychiatry*, 139, 338-340, March 1982.

Schertz, F., *"Taking Sides in the Unmarried Mother's Conflict"* in *Journal of Social Casework*, 28, 57-61, 1947.

Slife, B., ed., (1998), *Taking Sides: Clashing Views on Controversial Psychological Issues*, Tenth edition, Dushkin/McGraw Hill, Guilford, Connecticut, 1998.

Solinger, R., *Abortion Wars - A Half Century to Struggle 1950-2000*, University of California Press, Berkeley, California, 1998.

Solinger, R., *Wake Up Little Susie: Single Pregnancy and Race Before Roe v. Wade*, Routledge, New York, 1992.

Soll, J., *Adoption Healing*, Gateway Press, Baltimore, Maryland, 2000.

Sorosky, A., Baran, A., & Pannor, R., *The Adoption Triangle*, Anchor Press/Doubleday, New York, 1978.

Stiffler, L., *Synchronicity and Reunion*, FEA Publishing, Hobe Sound, Florida, 1992.

Taylor, P. E., *Shadow Train*, Gateway Press, Baltimore, Maryland, 1995.

Teller, Delores, *Shame on Us: How Shame Affects the Sexuality and Intimacy of Birthmothers*. Presented at American Adoption Congress Southwest Regional Conference, San Francisco, California, November 1998.

Verrier, N., *The Primal Wound*, Gateway Press, Baltimore, Maryland, 1997.

Vought, J., *Post-Abortion Trauma*, Zondervan Publishing House, Grand Rapids, Michigan, 1991.

Waldron, J., *Giving Away Simone*, Times Books, New York, 1995.

Wegar, K., *Adoption Identity and Kinship*, Yale University, New Haven, Connecticut, 1997.

Weintraub, M. & Konstam, V., "Birthmothers: Silent Relationships" in *Journal of Women and Social Work*, 10(3), Fall.

Wolff, J., *Secret Thoughts of An Adoptive Mother*, Andrews & McMeel, Kansas City, 1997.

Young L., *Out of Wedlock*, McGraw Hill, New York, 1954.

GLOSSARY

Adoptee - an adopted person of any age.

Adoption triad - the adoptee, the adoptive parents and the birth parents.

Agency adoption - licensed organization arranges adoption; the agency assumes guardianship until the final court hearing.

Amended birth certificate - an altered certificate of birth issued when the adoption is finalized. The names of the birth parents have been deleted; the names of the adoptive parents are recorded as the couple to whom the child is born.

Birth parent - term for mother and/or father of a child who has been relinquished for adoption (sometimes written as one word).

Closed adoption - also called confidential adoption. No information is shared between birth and adoptive parents.

Florence Crittenden Association of America - one of the two largest maternity home chains post World War II (the other was run by the Salvation Army).

Independent adoption - also called private adoption. Rather than a licensed agency, another entity, usually a physician or attorney, arranges the adoption.

International Soundex Reunion Registry - the largest non-profit, international registry. This free registry serves adults who have been separated by adoption or other circumstances including foster care and divorce. Registration forms are available at ISRR, P.O. Box 2312, Carson City, NV 89702.

Open adoption - information is shared between birth parents and adoptive parents; there may be ongoing communication between birth and adoptive parents. There is a wide range of "openness" in this type of adoption.

Open records - would allow the adoptee access to the original birth certificate (rather than just the amended birth certificate) as well as medical records pertaining to his or her birth.

Original birth certificate - records the birth parents' names and the name given to the child by the birth parent(s).

Private adoption - also called independent adoption.

Relinquishment - the legal termination of parental rights.

Reunion - re-establishment of contact between adoptee and birth parent.

Sealed records - records identifying the adopted person's birth parents and other information pertaining to the adoption proceedings are closed and made unavailable to the adoptee, the birth parents, and the adoptive parents. An amended certificate of birth is issued instead.

Search - the process by which the adoptee and/or the birth parent attempts to locate the other.

Surrender - another term for relinquishment; preferred term by many birth mothers who feel it more aptly describes their experience.

ABOUT THE AUTHOR

LYNNE REYMAN has taught and lectured widely in the area of assessment and treatment of child abuse and neglect. For many years she was a social worker and supervisor in Children's Services. She holds a Ph.D. in Psychology and is currently a Licensed Marriage and Family Therapist. *Musings of a Ghost Mother* synthesizes her personal reflections as a mother reunited with the daughter she surrendered for adoption and relevant literature regarding the impact of closed adoption on the life of the birth mother. She lives with her husband in Chico, California where she has a private practice.

❀

NOTES

NOTES

NOTES

NOTES

NOTES

NOTES